MANAGING APARTMENTS FOR PROFIT

Tips and Tricks for Taking Over and Managing Apartments

Alex Oliver
Emily Oliver

Dedication:

Thank you to our family and friends who helped make this book possible.

And to all the people who help our dream of real-estate investing come true.

Table of Contents

ATTENTION:

A Special Note about How this Book was Created.

Dear Apartment Investors,

Thank you for claiming your copy of ***MANAGING APARTMENTS FOR PROFIT: Tips and Tricks for Taking Over and Managing Apartments***.

This book will teach you critical apartment investing skills, tools, techniques and more that every apartment investor needs to understand and apply.

This book was originally created as a live interview. That's why it <u>reads as a conversation</u> rather than a traditional "book" that talks "at" you.

We want you to feel as though we are talking "with" you, much like a close friend or relative. We believe that creating the material this way will make it easier for you to grasp the topics and put them to use quickly.
We have also labeled each section to help you jump around to what you need.

So, relax.

Grab a pen or pencil and some paper to take notes as we talk you through the detailed ins and outs of how to be a successful apartment investor.

Sincerely,
Alex & Emily Oliver

<u>Our Background</u>

You can trust us and the information we are about to share because we have been successful apartment investors for more than 10 years. We started out with just a desire to invest. Then, through seminars, classes, talking to people and hard knocks we learned how to invest in apartments successfully. Since we managed our own properties from the beginning, we now know the ins and outs of how to acquire them, how to manage them and how to run them. We are excited to share what we have learned with you.

Hi everyone and welcome to your apartment investing roadmap. We are Emily and Alex Oliver, your apartment investing experts here to discuss the steps that every apartment investor needs to follow to get the best results and succeed with apartment investing. Welcome!

We will start with a little bit about our background and experience, so you can understand who we are, where we come from, and how we can relate to where you are right now.

Actually, neither of us have a background in real estate or business. We both went to school to study Mechanical Engineering. Alex focused on robotics, and loved the logic that robots follow. Whatever the input there is always a guaranteed output. There is a term that we used while in school, garbage in – garbage out. This logical thinking has helped both of us with real estate deals. Alex was very close to staying in school for many more years to focus on robotics and become a professor. However, instead Alex decided that he was ready to enter the working world and took a corporate job after graduation.

The job Alex took out of college was part of a leadership development program that moved us around the country. Every year or so we would move to a different city and work on various projects. Some of the projects saved his company millions of dollars, but we never saw any of that money. That was when we realized that very few people get rich working for large companies. Then in 2006 the company Alex worked for moved us to St. Louis, Missouri and that's when we started our real estate career.

Some might think that this was a terrible time to start investing. No one remembers the 2008 crash more than us, but we found that having experience in so many different market conditions has helped us better understand the basic principles of apartment investing and be able to share these lessons with you.

A lot of people wonder if we have taken any formal training relating to apartment investing. The answer is yes and no. Like many real estate investors, especially when you're coming from a corporate world, we went to a lot of investment seminars on various subjects including probate, flipping, stock investing, starting a business, and wholesaling, just to name a few. After sorting through all the information, we found the niche of apartment investing made the most sense for us. It really is a business to manage. Then Alex went to the St. Louis Apartment Association to become a certified apartment manager and enhance his skills. Overall, we have learned a lot on the job, but also try to incorporate any education that is available in order to enhance our knowledge.

To let you know where we started, as beginning apartment investors in early 2009, Alex had to call 27 banks before we found one that would finance our first building. This was when the market was down, and banks were very hesitant to do any apartment financing. Once we got the financing, however, within nine months we were able to get back all the initial cash plus some extra.

Now after years of experience, many successful projects and a lot of learning and hard work, we are ready to share what we know to help you find your success in apartment investing.

SECTION 1:

TAKING OVER APARTMENT BUILDINGS

Our Past Experience

Over the years we have purchased a wide variety of buildings. Some buildings were already running smoothly and just needed minor improvements. Others we went in knowing we needed to clean house. In many cases the last owners were distressed or just unaware and had not been managing the property well. That was our biggest value added. We could take over and start managing the property in a better way, including removing the residents that were causing problems by not paying their rent, disturbing their neighbors or other unacceptable actions. Especially because at the beginning we did all this ourselves, we really understand the ins and outs, and ups and downs of taking over buildings.

We were fortunate because our first building ended up working well for us but in the beginning, there were a lot of struggles. For our very first building Alex had to call 27 different banks to find someone who would finance the deal. (You can read more about this challenge and what we learned from it in our previous book _Finding and Financing Apartment Buildings_ which is available at Amazon.). It was a smaller 16 unit building and we ended up either evicting or at least terminating and moving out, 12 of those 16 tenants within the first six months. It was a trial by fire, but it was absolutely the right thing to do for the property. All our efforts did work out because within nine months of the purchase we were able to stabilize the building and recover all the cash that we put in plus some extra.

With that first purchase we learned quickly that you can't waste time when you need to do something to change the operations of an apartment building. From that start we have continued to build. We don't like to call ourselves an overnight success, but we have been very successful over the 10 years we have been in business.

Before You Even Close

The Plan

Before you even take over a new building, it's important to identify what you're going to do with the building once you get it. It is important to know, "Hey, here's what I'm planning on doing within the first couple days, within the first couple weeks, and within the first couple months." This is especially important if you're planning to do a lot of dramatic changes.

As part of your purchasing decision, you probably will have already identified what will get you the biggest bang for your buck, but now you need to get down to the details with timing and logistics. You want to have your contractors and others who will actually do the work lined up, so when you take over, they're ready to step in and start on day one. Getting started right away is important, as you will see from the rest of this book.

Standards, Rules, Policies and Procedures

The sooner you know the general policies and procedures for your new building, the easier it will be to enforce and the quicker you will get control of what is happening.

If this is your first building, you need to spend some time on this.

If this is not your first building, you should already have a start with the rules you had for your previous buildings. You will need to customize your policies and procedures to this new building, but you won't need to start from scratch. (For example: this building may have a parking lot where your others did not.)

For much more detailed information on this topic turn to the section in this book called, "Setting Your Standards, Rules, Policies and Procedures."

<u>Step One After Closing:</u>

Let Them Know There is a New Shariff in Town

The key when taking over an apartment building as a property manager, or as a self-managing apartment investor, regardless of the size of the property, is you must notify everybody. Not everyone's going know that you're the new owner or you're the new management company. It is absolutely critical to give everybody notice that you're the "new sheriff in town," the date that it is effective, and give them all your contact information. Who do they call for maintenance? Who do they call with rent questions? Who do they call for noise complaints or disturbances or there's a car in their parking spot? They need to know who to contact for all their concerns and maintenance issues.

They also need other details. Where do they send their rent now? Do they mail it in? Do they pay it online? How do they pay online if they do? What date are the changes taking effect? Is that going to be the first of next month? What if they still owe a balance, do they send it to you? So, you've got to make sure you get them notified immediately and completely - as soon as you take over the property.

We have seen so many management companies and apartment investors that delay on this step and it's disastrous. When there's a gap in contact information, when anybody needs to get hold of somebody, when it comes to having a maintenance issue especially, not knowing who to contact can create lots of problems.

If it is the middle of the month, you might not think it's important. After all, they're not sending their rent till the first of next month, so you figure you have a couple days to figure out how you will notify them. Well, let's say that a maintenance issues come up. If the residents don't have anybody to call, they will call the old company. The prior company will say they are not involved with the building anymore. Suddenly the resident is confused or unsure of who's going be fixing the problems for their property. Now, you've also got a problem with things that aren't getting fixed.

Another good example of this relates to one property we took over. We completed the closing signed all the documents and everything went well. We went to the property about two to three hours after closing, taped up notifications of a new owner along with our information. That night around 5 or 6 PM, after we taped up the notifications, the old owner came back to the building and started demanding rent from people saying that they had to pay their past-due rent and in some cases were asking for rent for next month saying they need to pre-pay.

In this case, the old owner was trying to scam the tenants out of money. However, because we put up the notifications, the tenants instantly called us, said somebody came to their door demanding money and even asked them to prepay which they normally don't do. The tenants were very confused and worried about what was happening. We let them know not to pay the previous owner. The closing documents have already been issued. Once the close has occurred, the tenants no longer owe money to the previous owner. Any back-due rent would be due to us, not the old owner.

So, in that case, the old owner was just trying to scam the tenants. Because we had properly and in a timely manner, notified the tenants of the change in ownership, we were able to help prevent the scam. If the tenants would have paid, they would have still owed us the same money and just been cheated by the prior owner.

How to Notify

It's best to have a printed letter notifying everybody that, effective of this date this is the new management company. You will want to provide a quick summary of contact info, so they know – "for maintenance contact here," "for management issues contact here." Maybe it's all one number if you're a small operation or you have just a general office number. But make sure everyone's got that contact information and then let them know you will be following up with each tenant individually if there are things that needs to be addressed.

The best way to notify tenants in your new building is to physically give them this notice when you take over. You need to go to the building physically. We know it's very convenient with our modern technology to think, "I don't really need to go because the last management company or the last owners gave me everyone's email address or phone numbers or whatever it may be." You don't know if that information is accurate and up to date. That may be their junk mail folder or their junk mail email address that they never really check. That may be an old cellphone number, or even a roommate's, a girlfriend's, somebody else's cell phone number. You can't guarantee they receive your information if you do it electronically.

If you physically deliver the letter, you know they received it the same day you took over. It's not going to be when they check their email two days later or when they get an anonymous text and they say, "Who is this?" A text saying hey we're the new owner of your building or we're the new management company, you need to call us for your maintenance issues does not feel very official.

Depending on the circumstances, you might also send the notices through the mail. This also makes it feel official. This may take longer so, especially if this is a foreclosure, you need to get something on the doors right away - but you could send mail as well. It generally best, however, to use postal mail as an additional notice, not as the only notice.

In addition, you can attach a sheet, requesting information from them. You can ask them to fill out what you need and return it to your office, mail it back or even email it to you.

Start with their contact information including their name, the best phone number where you can reach them, the best email, and an emergency contact name and phone number. This will get you their most current information.

It is also a good idea to ask what their rent is and how much of a security deposit they paid. In theory, you should have gotten copies of all the leases in advance, so you know exactly what their leases state. This is more critical in a situation where it's a foreclosure and you don't have documentation, or the last owner was not good at keeping documentation. That makes it very important. But it's not a bad idea no matter what, as a verification. You can make sure that what they're expecting and what the last owner and management company said, all match up.

This information request sheet is also a good opportunity to ask if there are any pressing maintenance concerns that need to be addressed. They may think that because they reported a maintenance issue to the last management company, they don't need to tell you. However, if the previous management company didn't transfer that information to you, you will not know. Without this information, it is possible that a week or two after you've taken over, you've got a really irate resident saying, "this has never been fixed." So, this is another good thing to request on the sheet. Remember the sheet needs to be easy for them to fill out and get it back to you.

You may find a lot of tenants saying, "Well, don't you already have this information?" You can respond by saying, "We just want to cross-reference it and make sure that everything is accurate during the transfer." You may even be able to preempt this by wording the request on your form that you're just trying to verify their information. You could start by saying something like, "We just want to clarify. What do you think you owe us in rent? How much did you give for a security deposit? What maintenance issues do you have?"

Also, with the request for maintenance information, they are more likely to send it back if you say something like, "We did not receive any notification of any maintenance issues for this apartment, please let us know if there is anything that needs to be done." Especially if the apartment was previously mismanaged, a lot of tenants are going have issues.

Not everyone will send information back and that's fine. It's just an opportunity to try to learn as much as possible, to let them know there is a new manager and to show them you want to do a good job with their building. Be proactive about collecting accurate information about your new building and its residents. You will probably get a lot more specific info than what the prior owner gave you.

In addition to the change of management notice and the request for information sheet, it is helpful if you can add a letter from the prior owner. If the prior owner or management company was fairly professional, so it's not a foreclosure situation, you can request a letter from them. This letter would state that they are ceasing management, or they no longer own the property as of X date. They might want to post their own letter, or you can post their letter with yours. This makes it a little clearer and more official that the ownership has changed. The tenant gets a letter from you and a letter from the prior owners/managers. So that way if the tenant has any questions, they can see it's official. The renter can contact the prior owner and get the same information. "Nope, we no longer manage that building. All your rent and security deposits and everything has been transferred to the new owners."

Be sure to include your contact information on one sheet for them to keep and anything you wish to have returned on a separate sheet. You can staple these sheets together along with the letter from the former building owner and possibly your new standards, rules, policies and procedures. Then you just have one packet to tape to the door. Make it easy for them to return the requested info to you and still keep a sheet so they can contact you with any needs or questions in the future.

How Much Time Should You Spend?

How much time it takes depends on the size of the property and the prior management. Especially with a bigger property, you don't have to address a letter to each one of them personally. It can be a form letter, "Attention all residents of," ... whatever the address or the name of the complex. It just needs to be clearly identified. You can have those all pre-printed if you've got 40 apartments, print off 40 plus a few more of the letters.

The delivery time will vary depending on the circumstances. We like to actually go around and put them on each door. So, if it's a mid-sized building, 20-40 units, you could spend a couple hours doing it. Some of it will depend on if you're wanting to actually introduce yourself to the residents when you leave the information. If you're knocking on doors and wanting to talk to them about the switch, then it might take a few more hours.

If it is a fairly clean and easy transfer of the property from the prior owner to you, then it might be fine just to drop the information door-to-door. If it is a foreclosure, like the example we already shared, you might be concerned about the prior owner coming back and claiming they still own the building. Then you'll probably want to be more aggressive with knocking on doors, letting people know there has been a change, letting them see your face and introducing yourself. If it has been a well-run building and you just need to let people know the new contact information and verify some of their info, then it is much easier. You can just go around and tape it on front doors.

It doesn't take a ton of time. Pre-print all the letters and then as soon as you leave the closing or if you're just taking over the management, as soon as the management contract is signed and everything's official, head straight over there and make sure people know about the changes right away.

It's also a good idea to print a couple extra information packets – more than the number of doors you have. That way, if anything happens you have a few extra. You might run into somebody and they say, "Well what is this?" You have an extra one to hand to them and you're not running short when you actually get to the final door.

Remember to put notices on all the common doors as well. Common doors would be things like, exterior doors that lead into a general hallway, a door to a stairwell that goes to multiple apartments, a general front door, or a back door. If the units don't have their own exterior doors, then there will be some type of exterior or "common" doors.

Some Examples

A good example of this is the one we gave earlier. When we were purchasing a foreclosure, it was good that we got the information out immediately after taking over.

Because it was a foreclosure purchase, the last owner had lost the building and the bank had taken the property. The bank sold it off to us immediately so there was really no period of time with a sign that the bank had possession of the property. Therefore, the same day we took over, the prior owners found out that they officially had lost the property.

Right away they went around and tried to collect rent. In this case it was very important to act immediately. We actually knocked on doors to catch as many people as could that were at home, so they would know, yes, the new owner is legitimate. Some people might get confused if they just find a letter on the door. If the building had been professionally managed, they might be used to getting notices on the door, but in a special case like this, personal and immediate contact made all the difference.

An example where this was not done very well was a property that we sold, and a new owner took over. He had a management company that was supposed to work for him. We got to know the new owner slightly during the process of the transition, so we had his contact info and talked to him just a couple times.

The building had been sold for about a week, but my property manager kept getting calls for maintenance. We told them that we didn't manage the building anymore and they needed to contact the new management company. And they would ask us, "Well, who is that?" So, they didn't know who to reach out to about maintenance issues. In addition, we got to the first of the next month and he had still not put out notices, so we started receiving rent checks from a property that we didn't even own or manage anymore. Now he's in a situation where the tenants don't know who to contact.

They've had maintenance issues that haven't been fixed in a month. They're sending in rent checks that are made out to the wrong management company so we're sending it back to them. Now the rent checks will be late, and the owner's not getting the rent checks that he's expecting to be get.

The tenants could also potentially be getting evicted. If the owner doesn't receive the rent check, the owner might start the eviction process when it was more just a misunderstanding of where to send the rent than it was really them not having paid the rent. This also creates bad feelings all around.

By the time he actually got in there with the management company - giving everybody notice, taking over, and starting to implement things, he had to dig himself out of a hole. He already had a couple residents that basically just moved out, they were like, "I can't get ahold of anybody. I can't get this maintenance issue fixed." We think it was a plumbing issue, so it was a fairly serious issue and they couldn't get hold of anybody. One previous tenant actually ran into our property manager at Subway as they were getting a sandwich, and they said, "Who in the world did you have take over this building because we can't get hold of anybody."

If you are not organized in getting out your information, it can cause chaos for you and your residents. Now you've started off with a bad situation where they don't trust you, they don't understand you, and they're upset.

You have to rebuild that relationship and that trust, at the same time you are trying to explain why they need to pay you the rent, and basically why they need to be good tenants. It is so much easier if you have started off on the right foot.

Another example of a situation that can arise is one where we had an irate tenant. In the records that we got from the prior owner, we had down that they had not paid a security deposit. They insisted they did. When they left, they did a good job cleaning up, so we did refund their security deposit even though we had no record anywhere that they were owed one. That meant that when we had closed with the previous owner, we didn't receive a credit for the security deposit.

It wasn't a very large amount. It wasn't large enough to go back and sue the previous owner for, but that is something that could happen. If the previous owner writes down zero security deposits for everybody and that's not actually the case, and the tenants do have security deposits, then you will have a bigger issue. This was a one-off case. Everyone else's was accurate. This was probably just either a mistake or something happened with the transfer. However, if every tenant had that issue, that would add up to a large sum of money and that would be something to watch out for.

So, in summary – you want to start off on the right foot

- Let your tenants know as soon as possible that the building has a new owner and/or property manager. If it is a foreclosure, you might even do this on the way home from the closing.

- Provide you tenants with all your contact information.
- Ask for their information, including any maintenance issues.
- If possible, add a letter from the former owner/manager to verify the change
- In some cases, especially if it was a poorly managed property, you might also attach a list of the rules under your ownership (See the section on "Setting Your Standards, Rules, Policies and Procedures.")
- Hand deliver this information stapled together either in person or by taping it to their doors.

Additional thoughts:

You need to follow through with whatever expectations you set so be careful not to overpromise. If you asked for maintenance issues and said you would get back to them personally, then you need to do that. Whatever you say you will do, be sure you make it happen or get back to them to explain why it didn't happen.

As you work with your tenants, you need to be clear with both them and yourself that some issues might be very important that you need to address on day one. Some of them might be something that you say "Okay, we'll add that to our list but it's going to be a week or two."

The good news is that the tenant can respond to you and then you can build up rapport with the tenant. Even if you have to say, "Alright we've received your note about this, it looks like this will probably be about two weeks out until we can fix it." the tenant knows, okay, you are doing something. When they know something will be happening with this issue then you are more likely to have satisfied tenants and they are more likely to let you know about maintenance issues that you should be taking care of. To keep the rapport, however, if you say you will get to that in 2 weeks, then you need to get to it in 2 weeks or let them know why it is not happening.

Step Two After Closing:

Fix Up What Everyone Sees First

The second step you do once you close on a building is to make a visual change, so it is clear there is new management in place. This is important because that's really what catches everyone's eye. That's what makes it very obvious that, "Oh, there is a new company here. This building has changed hands." So, it's important to make some sort of visual change at the property when you make that transition. The best way to do it really depends on exactly how much of a change you want to make in the operation of the building.

If it's a building that is in a serious state of disrepair and you are planning on a lot of changes like cleaning up the units and increasing rents, then you need a very quick, dramatic, visual change. Something on the exterior of the building with curb appeal. Landscaping is most common, but it could also be the entrances, the doors, exterior lighting. Something on the outside where someone driving by, or the residents when they come home, just say, "Wow look that this. They've already changed the look of this place. As soon as they came in, they started moving quickly." For the existing residents, it lends the sense that, "Okay, these guys are different than the last guys." If it was a building that needs a lot of change, they can say, "Okay, I see they are actually doing things." They can immediately see the change from the last owners who probably were not doing nearly as much, which is why it was distressed.

Some other things to consider updating to increase that WOW factor include common stairwells, common doorways and common hallways. Any area that people have to walk through to get to their apartments can start looking dingy and is one thing that owners often overlook. One or two fresh coats of paint in these areas can help the current tenants come in and think, "Wow. This looks fresh. This looks clean." As people move in or out, the walls get scuffed, there could be trash in the stairwells, so just doing a general clean-up and painting of common areas can make a big difference.

We would probably, however, make that secondary to the landscaping. The landscaping is something that everyone's going to see, the exterior is something that everyone's going see. That stairwell is definitely important, so we would do that after the landscaping, but you want to work your way from out, to in. Most important are the first impressions people see driving by, as they pull up to park, and as they start to walk up to the building. Make sure those are done first.

Then second, you should start going into the hallways, the stairwells, the common areas. You know, if it's just sweeping clean, obviously you can do that right away, but if you want to paint, maybe put in some new flooring, put in a different door, things like that, that would be in the follow-up steps. It is still in the same plan of your making some visual updates that change the look and feel of the building that, all in all, are not that expensive. You're not doing plumbing or electric or really heavy lifting on these things. Just relatively easy things like mowing, trimming and mulch make a big difference on the outside. On the inside, a coat of paint is also an easy way to make a big difference.

As you're trying to fill up the property, new people coming up will see this bright new exterior - the new landscaping or lights or doors. Whatever you decided to go with. It will make the building so much more appealing to current and potential residents.

If the building's already running fairly smoothly and less dramatic changes need to be made, then you don't need to spend as much time and energy doing something so dramatic. The change here could be something as small as, if there is a sign out front, making sure you've immediately updated that sign with your new contact number, management name and any other information. Maybe you could also do something small in a common area like the laundry room. Maybe you could just clean it up and put in some brighter lights. Other possibilities include putting some new flowers outside the leasing office, if it has an office, or repainting the office so it feels brighter. Do something that is going to be seen by everybody fairly quickly and that will reinforce, "Hey, we're the new guys in town." And now people can see, "Oh, wow, look. That did change. Hey, I wonder what's going on over there. That's really great."

So, making a quick visual change to the site is a very important second step in starting to establish that confidence and trust with the residents. It also helps you with your marketing and being able to fill vacancies.

How long does this step normally take?

How long it takes to make the first exterior changes, really depends. We've had some building where, within the first, probably, two weeks, we completely removed all the existing landscaping. The building had overgrown trees. We cut everything down, planted some new landscaping, put in a new retaining wall in front of the building and brought in some decorative landscaping rock. That one was a couple weeks, but it was a very dramatic couple weeks because it was a building where we really needed to make a change to the property. The property was in very rough shape. It had a worn-down exterior look and suddenly it had this bright, shiny, new look to it. So that one took a couple weeks.

There have been others where the buildings were in pretty good shape, so the biggest change was just getting a new sign put out front and cleaning it up. We had our landscaping guys there day one. We weren't doing a change in landscaping, but they did mowing, edging, new mulch, we planted a couple flowers, planted a couple things just to spruce it up a bit. That little bit made it look much fresher within the first couple days we were in there. It just had a freshened-up appearance. That doesn't cost a lot of money or time. We were going to have landscapers there anyway, we just had them do a little extra with the mulching, planting a few more flowers and making sure everything was trimmed up to look really sharp. It's amazing what landscaping will do to change the visual of a building, even if it's just a little more carefully done with mulch, plants, trims and things like that. It really makes a dramatic and positive visual impact.

You need to remember that the neighbors and other members of the general public didn't receive your notification letter about the new owner and/or management company. The only way they know there is a new owner is to see something change. So, if they had a bad experience with the old owners or they think it's maybe not the best-run building or they think the building is dated, your best way to deliver the message to them is to make some sort of exterior change. By making a visual change you make a statement. Now people look at your building and think, "Hey, look, there was a new sign that went up. Wow, I noticed the landscaping, it looks a lot sharper. Oh, all their doors are now a different color of paint."

It gets you attention, which is a very important thing. That's your message to the outside world that, yes, this is a new business, this is a new management company. In addition, if you do have a sign on the outside of it, the building is your billboard. You put, "Managed by" or "Property Management" or "Owned by" on the exterior with your name, contact number. You want it to look sharp because that's your billboard. You don't want people to say, "Oh man, look at that building that's managed by so-and-so, it sure does look run-down, doesn't it?" Having an up to date, nice sign is your best chance to make that very quick visual change and get people to notice. "Oh man, those guys came in, put in their sign ... That place looks like a million bucks."

Step Three After Closing:

Start Your Marketing

As a company, if you have multiple buildings, you always need to keep your company name out there and market to your potential residents.

Now, however, you have a new building. You've made a visual change so people on the outside world see that the building looks different. You're starting to enforce the policies and rules. You are changing the expectations. Now you need to get your marketing rolling for that building.

Start by getting some pictures of the units out into the public. Get your name and contact information out there so people can find you. Even if you don't have an empty apartment today, when you do have one, you've already got some marketing set up, you've already got your promotions going. You're also now overriding all the info that's out there with the old owner's contact information. So, the more you post, then people will see your contact info when they find that apartment or find that building. They'll know which number to contact because you've updated all your marketing materials, all your contact information and you have some online posts. So, as soon as you get past the first couple hurdles, make sure to get your marketing rolling.

Setting Your Standards, Rules, Policies and Procedures

It is important to immediately make clear your policies and procedures with the existing residents and new residents. The good news about this is that after you have one building you will already have the basic list of what you expect. Each new building will just require some customizing.

After you've given everyone notice and you're starting to make the outside changes, now you need to really enforce the policies and procedures that you have as a company and/or that you have in place in your leases. It's very easy, sometimes, to be a bit too lenient as people are transitioning from an old company to a new one. They're not used to the contact info and they want to do things the old way. You very quickly have to set the standards and expectations.

So, first consider their expectations of you. How quickly do you respond to maintenance issues? If they send in a request and it takes you a week to get to it, you've now set the expectation that you're slow to respond to maintenance needs. You need to make sure you're delivering on their expectations of you.

This then leads to your expectations from them. When it comes to the first of the month, are you ensuring that the rent is paid? Have you given them accurate information on where to pay? Have you made it easy for them to pay? It may be done online or through some sort of portal. Maybe you have some sort of physical drop-box. Determine the best way to make sure rent is collected on time and if it's not, follow up immediately. If it is not paid on time, maybe the last management company let people linger along and didn't really enforce collections. Make sure you're enforcing collections and enforcing late fees, along with making it easy for them to pay.

Finally, there are general policies and procedures. Are you keeping the place clean? The tenants will see that you are maintaining high standards for the building. Then, are you maintaining high standards from the residents? Are you not allowing people to work on their car in the parking lot and/or getting that broken-down vehicle out of the parking area? We don't allow residents to park a broken car on our lot. Are you addressing disturbance issues like people playing loud music at night? Are you addressing tenant complaints? Really set the standard at the beginning that you address things quickly, that you expect them to be respectful of each other, be respectful of the property, and that you're going to respond to things in a rapid fashion - from a maintenance side, from a resident side, from a rent side. That really reinforces the fact that you are proactive. It will set that standard. It will show that this is the new way of doing business and the old way is gone.

Also, don't be afraid of involving the police if need be. Some places where we own our properties, if you get more than two police calls in the revolving 12-month period, you're put on a list of nuisance property owners. However, because we have utilized the police, the nuisance property owner enforcer knows us and knows what we do if there is a police call. If there's an owner and he is not taking care of things, that owner may not want anyone to call the police. We've actually taken over buildings where the previous owner had told the tenants,

"Don't call the police. Whatever you do, don't call the police."

Then when we come in they know that we take care of things. There have been times when they call us and report things that really are police issues like fights on the property, or other problems. We tell them go ahead and call the police and we accept the fact that if we have more than two, we will be a nuisance property owner.

However, if we have police calls then we're able to get some of those tenants out because there's an easier eviction process for people who have had the police called on them or are causing issues. Then, because we do take action to evict the trouble-making tenants, the nuisance property officer gets to know us and know that we are making progress and taking steps in the right direction. They understand the direction we are taking and is willing to work with us. So, if there is something in your city that says you're a nuisance property owner, that Isn't necessarily a bad thing. Just turn it to your advantage. Your current residents and your community will eventually thank you.

Why Are Rules Important?

This is all about the mentality of, "Do you want to manage the building, or do you want to have the building manage you?" If you get out in front of it and set clear standards and expectations, then you can change the way the building is run. A perfect example is our building where the last owner let the tenants pay their rent when they wanted. They would come to the office every day. It was only 40 units, so it was not a big enough complex to afford having a manager sit in an office, eight hours a day, waiting for someone to show up to pay the rent. That expectation by the residents was very inefficient for us. In that case we provided a few options including paying online or mailing the check to our PO Box. This really helped us get the rent without having a person on site every day, and also helped the tenants to pay on time.

If you let the building manage you, you could be in the middle of the month and not have any rent collected. Then you have to go around and knock on everyone's door. That takes a ton of time and energy to get the rent that legally they're obligated to pay. That's why it's important to set these standards and expectations quickly and then follow through.

Just like the visual change, standards and rules are more important the more you need to change about the complex. If there's something really wrong because the last management company wasn't an active management company and let a lot of things slide, you need to be very proactive and quickly address these things. If you don't get right on it and follow through, you will have the building managing you and never get ahead of it. You're going to be chasing it for a long time. If you set the expectations and standards, and consistently follow them, then you'll find that a time-consuming, troublesome property can become a really well-run building. It's not quick or easy, but it is well worth the time and energy to do it.

Enforcing New Rules

The best way to take this step is by just being consistent and following up. So, if someone has a request into you, say on maintenance, or a complaint about something, or a problem with something broken in the building, you need to address it quickly. By addressing it right away you're setting that standard of, "Yes, we address things right away. We don't tolerate things lingering, both from a physical building standpoint and also, from a resident standpoint. We don't tolerate late fees lingering, we don't tolerate not following the policies and procedures that we have in place."

So, this is not a quick, one-time fix. This is a longer-term step. This isn't something you'll do once and be done with it. This is something that's ongoing. You're just consistently making sure you're maintaining those high standards, you're setting the high expectations, and following up to make sure the residents are abiding by the expectations, as well. A lot of times, you'll find that if you're maintaining your high standards, following up on maintenance requests, following up on resident complaints or issues or disturbances or whatever else it may be, that the residents will notice, "Oh wow, this building really is run more tightly," and it will impact the way they view the property as well. "I guess it is really important to make sure that I am more respectful. I'm not throwing trash on the ground because I'm not just adding to all the other trash that's already there." When the site is clean, and everything is well-maintained, people are less prone to abuse the building because it doesn't look abused.

So, it's just being consistent and communicating clearly, making sure they've got an easy path to get you information or requests. Especially when you first take over, though, generally you'll find, even in a well-maintained building, there's always small stuff that the last management company missed and there's a good chance for you to get a quick win. Residents can see, "Oh hey, this was never taken care of. Or this was going to be taken care of, but they never got around to it." If you come in and do that right away, you've won a lot of goodwill from the residents. They will say, "Okay, yeah. They do take care of their stuff. They did the stuff that the last guys never got around to."

Implement the New Standards

For us, it takes a couple months to get everybody transitioned to the new policies.

Here is an example of a building that was semi-professionally managed prior to us. It was a 40-unit complex. The last owners had owned it and self-managed it for about, 20 years. It was a retired guy and this was his retirement project. Because he was retired, he had a lot of time. It was an investment, but he had a ton of time to spend over there.

So, our very first month we were working on collecting rent. Everyone was used to being able to pay cash and being able to just come into the office at any time throughout the first 10 days of the month and drop off the rent. And, if there was no one in the office, then it was okay not to pay the rent that day. Also, if we didn't show up and knock on their door, that meant it was also okay to not pay the rent that day. So, it was very critical, for us at that building, to quickly put in place our policies and procedures around the rent. Here are your options to pay online. No, we don't take cash because from a security standpoint, we do not want to take cash.

From a record-keeping stand-point, if you hand me cash, there's no proof of this transaction happening. You could claim you gave me $600 and we say you gave me $500 or vice versa. You know, you pay me too much and we just don't credit it to your account. Is a risk that could happen. Or we lose track of how much you gave me. We don't know everybody at this building yet, so if some guy just walks up and says, "Hey, here's my rent." well, which apartment number are you in? Is this the right amount? We don't even know if you're paying me the right amount. We really wanted to get away from that as quickly as possible.

So, we had quite a few people we transitioned the first month, a little more the second month, and by the third month we pretty much had everyone flipped over. Now in that building about 90-some percent of the residents pay online and a handful actually still mail in a payment. The good news is, there's no physical going to the building and knocking on doors or sitting in the office, waiting for someone just to show up and drop off a rent check.

So, it depends on how much you have to change, but within the first three months you'll notice a real difference in the expectation if you're staying consistent. If you're reinforcing the rules and policies, it'll stick pretty quickly.

** Also see the tools section to learn about specific software that helps us with all of this.

About Leases and Continuity

Leases can be tricky and laws vary from state to state, so be sure to consult with your local attorney. With that understanding here are some general things to consider.

If you are not familiar with leases they are an agreement between the person wanting to live in the property and the owner or management company. It is set for a certain period of time (usually a year), and defines a periodic (usually one month) rent plus an agreement with your expected standards. There are positives and downsides for both parties. The rent is set for the resident so they don't have to worry about a rent increase but there is usually a defined penalty if they "break" the lease and leave early. The owner or management company has a commitment from a resident to stay a certain amount of time, but the rent cannot be changed during that timeframe. You can find standard leasing forms online, but it is always best to consult your attorney.

Generally, when you take over a building, you will already have a lease for each apartment from the prior owner and normally you are required to honor that lease until the lease end date because a lease is a legal contract.

As a legal document, it is binding on the resident and the lessor, whether it be the management company or the owner, to abide by this lease. Leases are affected by state laws, so you would need to confirm with attorneys on this, but they are usually fully transferable upon a sale. So, with a normal sale, or even if it's through one management company being transferred to a different management company, the leases are also transferred, and these are still legally binding documents.

When you first take over the property, if there's an existing lease with a remaining term, then both you and the tenant are still bound to honor the terms of the lease. It has just been transferred to the new management company or the new owner, whichever way it may be. For example, if you take over in July and the lease runs through December, you have six months left on that person's lease.

Now when their lease does expire, you obviously would like to put them on a new lease. That will be a chance to renew them with your lease, your terms, your policies, your legal standing.

Some companies, however, either because of lax management or by policy, will automatically roll any expired lease to a month-to-month type agreement. If you have tenants in your new building that are in this month to month type of agreement, then the very first day you get in there, you can sign a new lease with them that sets up new terms and includes agreement to your standards. If it is not month to month, you are bound by the old lease until it expires. Now, again, this can get into some legal stuff so definitely ask your attorney.

In some states, when there is a foreclosure, the foreclosure supersedes the lease. This means leases are, in essence, voided by the foreclosure process. You'll also find, during a foreclosure, usually the tenants' security deposits are either lost to the previous owner or given to the bank. They are usually not passed on to you, the new buyer. Basically, everything is terminated at the bank because the last owner had the money and didn't give it to anybody. (If there are residents who moved in after the foreclosure took place they would be a different story.) If you have this situation you should definitely talk to a 'Landlord Tenant Law' specializing attorney, especially for your state. Different states have different rules.

So, it could very easily take 12 months to turn the tenants over to your leases. If the past company was maintaining lease renewals, then every time a lease expires they should be signing a new, probably a 12-month renewal. It could even take more than 12 months if they happen to do longer leases. It's likely less urgent if they did longer leases because that means the past owner/manager was probably on top of their lease documentation. They might have intentionally signed 13 or 14-month leases to try to get a little longer time, or space out the renewal periods, or space out when there would be move-in's and move-out's. If that is the case, they probably had a pretty thorough lease, making it less urgent to change. So, if there is a year-long lease that was signed last month, meaning they are only one month into a 12-month period, then you have 11 months before you can switch them over to your lease.

So, what happens when they have not yet officially signed a lease with your new rules? For example, we have a clause in our leases that says, if you have a police call, there could potentially be an expedited eviction process. In other words, we don't have to wait for non-payment if there are police calls on a resident, before we begin evicting them. But what if the lease they have doesn't say that? Step three says enforce the rules, but how do you enforce rules if not everyone has the same rules on their lease?

Not all rules have to be in a lease. You'll want it in your lease too, I'm not saying you should **not** put that in your lease. But you can still enforce policies and rules without it being in a lease. If someone's disturbing the residents, you can say that disturbs other residents' legal rights to have peaceful occupancy of the residence. So, even though that person doesn't have lease clause specifically stating that rule, we can still say they are violating others legal right to have peaceful occupancy of their apartments.

It is the same with picking up trash or leaving junk cars in the parking lot. We can say, "Look, don't throw trash on the ground. I'm going charge you for trash on the ground." We can also put up a sign, and enforce it that says, "'No vehicles on this parking pad can be broken down, damaged or have expired plates. This is true for whatever policies you have on the property. They don't have to 100% of the time be on the lease in order to enforce them. We are not saying don't put them on your lease. This just relates to people who have not yet signed your lease. Again, consult with your attorney, but there are rules and policies that you can still enforce regardless of the lease.

There may be some things, depending on what their existing lease says, that might be easier or harder to enforce. For example, you may have a rule that there is no smoking in the units. If someone does that but that restriction is not stipulated in their current lease, that's going to be tougher to enforce. A noise complaint, on the other hand, might be easier to enforce, because now they are violating a fellow resident's legal rights. Of course, if they're doing some illegal activity, that's already an illegal activity so you can use the police or legal resources and say, "Hey, this is an illegal activity." It's not related to the lease. The tougher ones to enforce before you get new leases sighed are things like 'no smoking'.

Having said that, there are some things you cannot do. For example, if they have no clause that discusses late fees, you can't arbitrarily charge late fees. If the lease says they have till the 15th to pay rent, then they have till the 15th. It is important to read these leases when they are provided to you during your due diligence period before buying the building. Make sure you know what you are getting into, and what you will be legally required to abide until you can get people onto your lease.

But as far as talking to a resident, you can tell them this is the expectation. You can tell them they're not following rules and procedures. If you keep telling them and telling them and telling them, they're probably going to get the hint that this is not the expectation. This is not going to work. They are likely to get tired of you harassing them and they are either going change their ways or decide to move. So, it is far from ideal when take over a property that had a simple, one-page lease, but with time and persistence, you can switch it over to a well-run property.

The good news is, if it has been professionally managed, you really shouldn't encounter these problems at all. You usually only see this if it was a poorly managed complex. If it was a poorly managed complex, you might choose to talk with the resident and say, "Look, we really want to get a new lease going with you." You can negotiate. "We're going to set your rent at this, but we're also going fix up these three things that the last owner didn't do. So, let's get a new 12-month lease in place that's with us with these terms and that will override the old lease." Help them understand the value you are bringing to their living experience.

Whether you should wait or try to override the old lease depends on the validity of the prior lease – and the approval of your attorney. If they have a fairly solid lease, you do not have legal grounds to make them sign a new lease. So, unless there's a real issue that you need to address you might want to wait until the current lease is going to expire. Again, consult with your attorney.

Just as an FYI, we generally approach someone about renewing an existing lease, around 60 – 90 days prior to its expiration.

The Best Tools

We keep talking about management software. We actually use a web-based software that is called AppFolio. It's all online. The great thing about it is you can track so many different things. It's a full-blown property management software so you can keep track of things like delinquencies, making sure everyone's rent has been paid. It has a lot of options. People can pay online. They can pay with a credit card. They can make a direct payment from their bank account. There is also a cash payment option for residents that don't have bank accounts. They can take cash into a store, have them scan a barcode, and it will pay against their account. So, we give them a lot of options to set that expectation of, "No, it's really easy to make a payment. it's not hard to get rent to us," So this software makes managing rents easy.

AppFolio also helps with tracking maintenance. It is a big issue to keep track of those maintenance things, so you don't have stuff that gets missed. "Oh, so when Susie called in and told us about this thing last Monday we put it at the bottom of the priority list because it wasn't that urgent and now we forgot about it." By having a maintenance log, and the software will track that for you, you can see the maintenance request that was put in and what date it requested. That way you can make sure you don't get stuff that's lingering for too long.

It's also a great place where you can gather notes on residents. If someone has a noise complaint, you can document it in AppFolio, so you can go back and say, "Hey, you know, we've had three noise complaints from your neighbors in the last 30 days or 90 days, whatever it may be. It happened on this date, this date, and this date. That way you can be much more consistent with your documentation so it's not going purely by your memory. "Oh, well, I don't remember exactly when that happened, but I'm pretty sure it happened." If you can document it, it's critical for being able to follow up and maintain that standard.

We had a lawyer friend that told us "The one with the most documentation wins." So, if you're ever in a dispute or anyone ever contests what you're telling them, just make sure you've got your documentation. A high-quality management software is the best way to keep documentation all in one place. It keeps things consistent and it makes it easily accessible when you need to pull it up.

We had one woman we evicted, and she challenged us with a court case in front of a judge. She claimed that she had paid her rent every month on time and had the receipts to prove it. We also printed her rent history including all payments we received, rent changes, and late fees. When the court case arrived, she provided all of her receipts that matched exactly with our records. The judge could see that our records were accurate and that she had not been paying her rent. The judge ruled in our favor and she was evicted. If we wouldn't have had those records or if they wouldn't have matched her receipts, then everything could have been drawn out and she could have continued to live for free at our expense. This is just one of many examples of when good documentation is critical in resolving issues or disagreements quickly.

There are other tools besides AppFolio, but it's important to realize that, especially depending on the size of the building, not everything needs to be high-tech. When you're doing analysis on a building it can be through Excel. When you're preparing those letters for all the residents you can just use a Word document. Just type up a simple, generic letter. It doesn't have to be a fancy email with a link and a response. Sometimes we try to be too techie. There are a lot of times that just basic, offline, physical tools and physical letters work fine.

For some actions there may not even be an app - like for the visual part in the step two visual change. For verification that a transformation is being made it is important to go to the building and view the changes physically. If you have a maintenance crew or contractors doing the work, physically go there, see what's happening and keep an eye on the project. Not everything is going to be online.

Having said that, it is important to recognize that, especially if you have a bigger building, property management software is going to be very important. You don't know the residents and who is in which apartment. You don't know who's paying what. You don't know when their lease is expiring. So, rather than trying to keep track of all that through spreadsheets or manually, software can be very helpful.

What we really like about our software is it's all online, so we can just pull up on the phone when we are at a building and say, "Oh, yeah, this person in this unit ... Hey they only paid partial this month. I haven't gotten the rest of their rent, yet," or, "Oh, you know, yeah I do see they have a maintenance request that we haven't closed out."

So, online software is really a powerful tool. It may not necessarily be cheap, but it can keep you from chasing your tail. When we first started, we did a lot of stuff on spreadsheets and notepads. We would have notepad after notepad of maintenance requests. We'd write out the maintenance issue and when it was done there'd be a line drawn through it and we'd just keep adding to the sheets. The first 20 pages of the notepad were just lined out requests, but we could to go back and see if we hadn't lined it out yet. This was not a very efficient way of keeping track of maintenance issues. So, any sort of software or online tool that will help keep information in one place, is going to be really valuable in making the transition happen quickly and easily.

In addition to helping you, more modern systems can help and impress your residents. If the last owner was using a hand-written ledger to try to keep track of who owed what (we have seen this), there may have been a lot of confusion and inaccurate records. If you can come in and say, "Look, here's an online portal where you can submit maintenance requests, or you can pay your rent, where you can manage your renewals and you have access to copies of your leases," ... That's a very sophisticated update that a lot of residents would appreciate.

This wouldn't necessarily be a visual change but would definitely change how the existing residents would feel, and it would also be a way of saying, "Wow, look at the change that's happening. This company really knows what they're doing." The same effect would be true for new applicants as well. You are showing them that you are a high-tech company that is going to be responsive and easy to work with.

High Tech vs. Low Tech Tools

So, in review, sometimes we want to use new tools and sometimes the old. A paper letter, a physical notice, something printed and hanging on someone's door, and getting official mail will make a huge impression. A text or an email have become so commonplace that it's very easy to ignore and/or forget them. It's very easy not to see them. So, sometimes low-tech is the right way to go. It is also a really good way to have documentation. If you go "low tech" you have a physical copy, or you have an electronic copy that you've saved and then printed out. When you physically deliver a letter or notice, it can have a much more impact and feels much more official than just getting something electronically.

Time Wasters to Avoid

When considering the above suggestions, don't try to jump to step three or further, until you have completed both steps one and two. They are both critical!

A lot of apartment investors want to jump right into the interior or the apartments. They take over a building that's got one or two vacancies. They want to fix up that vacant unit and they're going to get that interior looking great. They are excited. "Oh man we're going to jump the rents really high and this is going to be an awesome return on our investment." They've forgotten to do the outside appearance first. Work your way from outside, in. It is so important to start out with that exterior visual change. Get that in place so people even come up to your building.

We know from experience. We can think of a few times when we first took over some properties that were in rough shape. Before we got that outside changed, we had people setting appointments to come look at the units. We didn't hear directly from them, but we were fairly confident we could see them slowing down in front of the building, taking a look, deciding it was not the building they wanted to live in, and continue driving down the street.

So, you must change that exterior appearance first so people know, "Oh yeah, this building does look pretty nice. I'm willing to come inside and take a look at that nice apartment you did." Until you've got that outside done, no one's even going to stop to see that really beautiful work you have done.

If you can't get people to come and look at your super awesome fixed up units then you have wasted a lot of time and money. You want people to drive by and want to live there, want to be part of your community.

Another big time waster is not putting up the notification of new ownership right away. Once you miss this step trying to go back is very difficult and takes a LOT more time than just posting signs the day of close. Once the rent is sent to the wrong company you now have to work with them to get a credit or have the tenant cancel the payment and reissue it to you. If someone moved out without you knowing you may need to formally evict them to legally gain back the right to the unit. Again, a much worse situation than just working with the tenant if they chose to move.

These are easily avoidable situations. If you do things properly you can save a ton of time and headache down the road.

The Biggest Challenges You Will Face

There are several challenges with taking over apartments, but a couple come immediately to mind.

The first we have already mentioned. Because we have so much technology, people want to do everything online or everything via text or everything via electronic communication. Relying too much on technology is a mistake and the investor needs to overcome that mentality.

In this day and age, it can be very challenging to slow down and physically go to the building. Or if you are buying a property that is in another city or state. There is a temptation just to send one email letter to everyone in the building. It is faster, easier, and much less of a hassle for you. But that is not the best thing for the tenants.

At the end of the day real estate is a people business. If you just bought a 30-unit apartment there are 30-60 people counting on you to help them through this transition, depending on the size of the units. They don't know who you are or what your company stands for. They don't know the new expectations or how to pay rent until you come in and help them understand.

If you want also to send them an email, and perhaps reference that in the letter you tape to the door, that is fine. But there needs to be some sort of physical touch with the tenants or you will be struggling for months to recover.

The other challenge is being able to address the confrontation and/or issues that come up from residents. "Hey, we just took over this building, people are complaining about this and that. Oh boy, I don't really want to deal with it." That is a true challenge. It's not fun to deal with those issues, but if you put them off, they are just going to get worse. You must address things right away when they happen, so they don't get worse and they don't get out of hand. You must address those things immediately even though it is difficult.

This is where having a team together before you start is important. Are you going to be fixing up the building yourself or will you have a team to help you? Know who you can call for small maintenance issues. Keep a list of issues that are reported so that you can prioritize and make sure everything gets done.

This challenge with taking over the property is short term. Once you go in and fix up what needs to be done you can then begin to follow your standard maintenance process. At the begging there are going to be a lot more calls, especially if the old owner didn't keep up with the building.

There is mental aspect of this challenge. Getting so many complaints can become overwhelming for you and your team. If you are not sure where to start then just make a list of all of the issues, with the tenant name and unit number. Also include the impact level to tenant. Is the water not working in the bathroom sink or is it just a drip? We had one property that we looked at taking over where the previous owner was using duct tape to fix plumbing issues. Needless to say whoever ended up buying that building would have had a very large list of maintenance issues when they first took over.

After you have your list it can be easier to prioritize them. Then you know who you need to call. Do you need a plumber, electrician, handyman, or can you do all of the work yourself? Once you know who is doing the work you can just start working on that list. Keep going until all of the issues have been addressed.

Getting over this challenge and working with the tenants to fix their issues will help build respect and rapport with the residents and at the same time benefit the property by functioning more smoothly. If you do a good job with the fixes you shouldn't need to come back and address that same issue later. Addressing issues and striving to be proactive instead of reactive is a big step in overcoming and preventing many difficulties.

The HUGE Opportunities

The biggest opportunity is that sometimes small and relatively inexpensive changes make a huge difference. When you make that little bit of outside landscaping update, it makes the whole building feel new and clean. If you have someone go through and mop and clean the hallways, or polish and scrub the floors so they have a nice shine, or maybe add some air fresheners, or put in some new, brighter light bulbs in the hallways or outside the building, you can make a huge change in peoples' perception of your property. These don't have to be dramatic. You may not need to rip everything out and put in brand new landscaping. A lot of times it's the little, small changes that really do make a big difference. You can make large changes in how people view your building and make it clear that there is new management in town, just by paying attention to the small details.

These small changes can also help your bottom line. If the last owner had the property at half full you may now be able to lease the remaining units. That is a direct impact on how much money you make and what the property is worth. There are some relatively small investments that can put more money in your pocket and increase the value of the building.

However, you need to make sure that you are budgeting for these expenses up front when you buy a building. Make sure that you are factoring in expenses for landscaping, updating common areas, and general fix-up of the property. Even if it looks in good shape during your inspection adding some new plants outside, changing the color of the hallways to a more modern look, or updating a sign can make a big difference. If you didn't set aside funds for this work, then you may have to pay for this out of cash flow. If the building if only half full and barely covering the mortgage, then you might not have the funds to do all of the work you need to in order to get the property fully leased.

We call this the "Romeo Spiral" because we knew an investor that got himself into a bad situation. All of his property ended up getting sold or foreclosed on. He didn't have enough money from cash flow to fix up his units properly, so he did a bad job. This included not fixing plumbing or roof issues. Therefore, he couldn't get good tenants who would pay rent.

They would pay their first 2 to 3 months' rent then stop paying. He would then have to pay to evict them, sometimes more then he even received in rent. So now instead of having more money because he leased the building he has less. So, he has less money to fix up the unit so the next person willing to move into the building is even worse. This goes on and on until the building is in disarray, the tenants have very low expectations, and the owner doesn't have the funds to get out of this mess. The only option is to sell or foreclose.

The good news is that this can lead to some good deals in the market. If you can find a seller who has just started down the spiral then you can come in and fix the issues and make the place look nice. This will be very different from the old owner so the tenants and neighbors will notice the difference.

Be careful with this step, however. If someone has fallen all the way to the bottom of the spiral, then their property may be too costly to fix up. If all of the plumbing has been 'fixed' with duct tape for several years that means that the flooring is bad, the sub floor is bad, the cabinet is bad, and possibly the joists are bad. That is a lot of fix up. So you will need to determine if the future rents will be worth the cost.

On the flip side, if the previous owner let the cosmetics slide so the building doesn't look pretty but all of the systems are solid then you can go in and make a huge difference without spending too much. This would be the ideal property to buy and the biggest bang for your buck.

The Best Mindset

The best mindset is, you want to be fast. You must make these changes very quickly. You only get one chance to make a first impression. So, by cleaning up that exterior, you are making that first impression on people coming in to look at the apartments. You are enforcing the rules; you're following your policies. This is your opportunity to make that first impression with the existing residents, but you've got to move fast across the board – informing the residents, fixing up the outside and responding to tenant issues including maintenance.

A few times we have fallen behind and took the attitude, "Oh well, you know, we're kind of busy right now." This meant that a couple things slipped through the cracks. it is amazing how quickly everyone notices that and now you're digging yourself back out of a hole. So, it's just a good philosophy to be fast and stay on top of things. Be quick to respond, quick to address issues, and be as proactive as possible. Which means it all comes down to speed, and organization can help you be speedy.

If you are struggling with getting into this mindset then take it one step at a time. Make a list of all of the items that need to be done, their cost, and who can do the work. As we said before, work from the outside in. If you are planning on doing all of the work yourself start with the landscaping. If you are in the middle of winter in New York, then maybe start with the common halls and focus on the landscaping in the spring. But the point is that you will have limited funds and time. You need to make sure you are spending both wisely while getting the biggest bang for your buck.

Once you have the list and it is properly prioritized then just start getting the work done. If you are hiring it out and this is your first time working with the crew, make sure to stop by often. say hello, walk around, see what they are doing. This also helps if they have any questions regarding the work. They may not want to 'bother' you with a phone call but if you are there, they will ask what you want. This also builds the relationship so they will begin to understand when they should call you and what decisions they can make on their own. This will make sure that you are getting what you want without being bothered for every small thing.

Keep in mind that at the core, real estate is a people business. The people paying their rent and paying your bills. Without them you couldn't afford to keep the building in good shape. The people doing the work are trying to feed their family and do a good job. You need to be clear with what you want and then follow-up to make sure they understand by stopping by and seeing how the work is going.

If you don't like interacting with people, then real estate may not be for you. This job is not one that can be done from behind a computer. And until you get much bigger there are a lot of benefits to investing close enough to home to be able to stop by and see the tenants or see the work being done.

So, the mindset that is the most helpful is people focused. If you are thinking about the people, then you will act quickly and work to keep the building up to your high standards. This will, in turn, get good tenants who will want to live in your building and working crews who know what to expect from you. Having a people focused mindset will help to pull all of the lessons of this book together and help you have a successfully apartment career.

Some Detailed Examples:

So, we have a couple of stories. They are similar to, or overlap some, with the ones we've told already but we think they are helpful to hear. One good example is the building we took over a couple years ago where it had been self-managed for 20 years. The residents were used to paying rent a certain way. They would just drop off cash whenever they came to the office.

Within a few months we were able to convert everyone from cash payments and paying whenever to paying on time and online. Also, we don't think the previous owner had ever enforced late fees even though they did have them in their leases. So, we started enforcing late fees and enforcing the expectation that rent needed to be paid on time.

We also really managed renewals. They had let a lot of their leases go month-to-month because they just felt, "Well, we don't really need to manage renewals." We managed the renewals, which got us some rent increases. We were able to fix up some stuff inside the building that they had not maintained in years. Some of the residents had been there 10+ years but the owner had never gone in to paint or do anything like that in exchange for never raising rents.

So, we averaged, within the first 12 months of owning that building, a $100-$150 rent increase per unit and only had, maybe, 5% of the residents move out in the process. Now somewhere between 80 and 90% of the rent is paid online and the rents are paid on time. The handful of rents that aren't paid online are mailed into a mailbox. We don't have to collect any of them physically. We've also been able to get higher occupancy.

Outside we did some minor things with landscaping like new mulch, but we also did something with the parking lot that made a big difference. We resealed and striped it. The parking lot was looking a little faded, starting to get some cracks but it wasn't really destroyed. It was a whole lot cheaper to reseal it than to let it go and repave it down the road. In addition, with resealing, you get a nice shiny feel. Then you add really bright yellow striping and suddenly it feels like a brand-new parking lot for a fraction of the cost of actually paving a brand-new parking lot. It is preemptive of trouble down the road and it makes the parking lot look amazing.

Again, it's a lot of those small things: new brighter lights in the stairwells that lead up to the apartments, cleaning up the laundry room, adding some brighter lights in there. It's those really small things that made a huge difference.

An example of something that did not go well was the time we sold a property that the owner did not go in there with his notices or make any visual changes to the exterior. It was not a great location. The building was in a lower income area. Unfortunately, there had been a fair amount of crime in the area, as well. We were managing the building pretty tightly. It took a lot of time and effort to manage it, but we kept it fairly well under control.

He took over, didn't notify anybody, I'm not even entirely sure if he really had a management company in place that was ready to take over on day one. Within three months he went from about 85-90% occupied to about 50% occupied. It was 18 apartments and almost half of them moved out within a few months just because things weren't getting fixed, things weren't getting taken care of and in that neighborhood, it started to become a security concern.

There would be a broken latch or a broken window at the entrance door to the stairwell. Suddenly, people who didn't live there could come inside the hallways at night. Some of the residents were not feeling safe and they didn't have anybody to contact or they weren't getting responses to their contacts, so they were moving out.

These stories are not meant to scare you. As long as you keep the people in mind and work hard to keep the property in good shape you can increase the rent, have people who want to move in, and be able to afford the changes necessary to keep everything running smoothly.

The owners in these cautionary tales didn't have the help or guidance like you do in order to make the most out of their real estate careers.

Time Management Tips

You need to prioritize your efforts. Focus on where you will get the biggest bang for your buck first and then work your way backwards. Don't waste a lot of time and money chasing really big things. Those small things are where get your biggest return. Knock those out first and then move on.

This goes back to starting on the outside and working your way in. For example, let us say that you buy a building and you focus a lot of time and money fixing up one unit with a new kitchen, updated bathroom and new flooring. Well, then when you go to rent that wonderful updated until people drive by, slow down and then keep driving. So, you spent a lot of time and money, but the quality people you want to rent from you won't even come in the door.

This exact situation has happened to us when we first started. That is why you should always start from the outside and work your way into the building. After you have paid so much money to fix up a unit you want to make sure it rents fast. Well a little time and money up front on the exterior will help you rent your unit faster.

Another time waster is focusing on the unimportant maintenance items first. If there is a problem that needs to be addressed, then you will need to make sure to take care of it.
However, keep in mind that not everything is a rush. If it is a Saturday or Sunday on a 75-degree day and someone's AC isn't work that can wait till Monday. Now if it is 110 degree or below freezing then it needs to be

addressed ASAP because that can cause an unsafe living condition.

The thing to remember is that just because it is reported today doesn't mean it has to be worked today. If someone reports that their sink is dripping, that can be fixed between 8-5 Monday through Friday. Now if someone reports a pipe burst and water is running down their apartment that needs to be fixed right away. When owner can't distinguish between the urgent and non-urgent, they can waste a lot of time and money calling in professionals on off hours for items that could have waited.

This goes back to setting good expectations with the tenants. They knew that we would get to their issue when we said we would. Because we had that trust, they would believe us if we said we would get to it first thing Monday. Often when we first take over a property that was mismanaged, before we had time to build a good relationship, the tenants would demand action right then. This is probably because with the past owner if they didn't take action right then it wouldn't get addressed at all.   Most people are reasonable if they know that you are going to do what you say you are going to do.

The final big time waster is setting the expectation with the tenants that you will be at the property every day. If you are retired and this is your hobby you may be fine with driving over and sitting in an office or walking around for hours. But if this is an investment and you want to grow then that model is not scalable. If you are in a situation where you feel you need to be in the office, or hire someone to be there, make sure to set specific hours so that the residents know when they can come in to pay the rent or put in a maintenance request. Otherwise you are wasting time and energy that could be used looking at other deals, spending time with family, or going on a vacation.

Don't give up your dreams to run your real estate property. Make sure to save time and money by fixing up the property from the outside in, schedule non-critical maintenance issues during normal business hours, and set clear expectations regarding how often you will be onsite. This will help you save time and money and you can continue your investing career.

Why This Is Easier Than Ever

What makes it easier than ever to take over an apartment building is that there are more tools for landlords. There are the web-based management tools and a lot more resources are available online to do your marketing and your promotions. You can also now do a lot more with virtual phone systems for getting responses to tenants. So, that tech side is very helpful.

When we first got into this business, we met a man who had started investing in the late 1970s or early 1980s. He listed his work phone on all of his signs because that is where we was most of the time. He would get the calls and schedule the appointments for after work. He boss got wind that he was getting so many calls for his real estate and decided to part ways (AKA he got fired).

We don't really realize how good we have it nowadays. We can have multiple numbers that all call to the same phone, or change phones depending on the time of day. We can hop on our phones and look up anything on the internet. We can take a call anywhere we are day or night. These tools are a huge help for apartment investors, especially those who are just starting out.

The trade-off is there are also a lot of high expectations from tenants. They expect to be able to do things online, they expect to be able to do things remotely. So, you've got to make sure you can deliver on those expectations. Provide options for online payments. Have a portal where tenants can submit maintenance requests. These tools make it easier for you and the residents. You are more likely to get the rent on time and learn about any issues with the building. You will also have a more professional feel to your management company. These are all things that good tenants will expecting but may not tell you about.

The good news for you is that getting your hands on these tools is easier than ever. There are many companies offering phone answering services, VOIP (voice over IP) services, or tenant services. The costs of these products have gone down dramatically as there is more competition in the market for your business. Use that to your advantage and find something that works for you and your business.

In addition to the tools it is easier than ever to see what your competition is up to. Although you may still need to make some phones calls to find out rent, square footage and condition of a building now most of that information can be found online. Simple searches can help you determine the average rent in an area and see pictures of the condition of neighboring buildings.

This can help you while buying the property to make sure that your rent estimates are in line and while you are trying to rent vacant units. There is nothing wrong with attempting to rent units at the top of the market, but it is good to know that is what you are doing before you begin. that will help you with your marketing and sales pitch when people stop by to look at your units.

The information about other building didn't use to be so easy to come by. We would have to call other buildings in the area acting like we were needing an apartment. If we wanted to see the condition, we had to schedule an appointment to see the unit. Now it is so much easier to see where your building falls within a neighborhood. We are truly living in a remarkable time.

Final Thoughts on Taking Over Buildings

A final thought is to just be proactive with your time. You can't create more of it. So, remember, you want to manage the building, not have the building manage you. Just think about it from the standpoint of where you're getting the best use of your time and money.

You also don't want to go through this process twice. You know, you don't want to try to take over once, misfire, and now you've got to go back through and try to get everybody back in line and readdress all these issues. Do it once, do it right the first time, and that way you're not doubling your efforts or going through twice the work. But with the information you have learned here you should have no problem focusing on what is important and do a great job taking over your apartment building.

As we said at the beginning, taking over apartment buildings is a business endeavor that can be fun and very rewarding. Hopefully, this section has given you some tips and a roadmap to help you get started when you take over apartments.

Have a great day!

SECTION 2:

EFFECTIVELY MANAGING YOUR BUILDING

Our Experience with Managing Apartments

We have been where you are and want to help you understand and avoid the most troublesome problems for investors.

We have been investing in apartment buildings since early 2009. In the beginning we did not have a management company, so we worked directly with the tenants, contractors, maintenance and even collections. We were personally involved with all aspects of managing our buildings so we truly understand all the issues that can arise.

Our first investment was a small four-unit building, that we purchased without any formal training. It was intimidating for us. We made a lot of mistakes in the way we handled those tenants. Knowing what we know now, we would have done things differently. The project ended up working out well, but the training and guidance in property management have really helped as we have gotten into larger apartment buildings with multiple tenants.

Once we started, we've grown rapidly and managed various types of properties. We have had properties in both lower and higher income areas. For some properties we were taking over a building that was poorly managed either by a management company or the owner. There were no standards or collection policies and, in some cases, not even any leases. Some properties had verbal leases, but nothing written. (Section 1 above gives more information about what to do when you first take over a property from a 'dead-beat' owner.)

Many of the buildings we purchased required some upgrading from minor repairs to major construction. One project required so much reconstruction that as soon as we took over, we had to relocate all the residents. For other projects we were able to upgrade one unit at a time. When a lease ended, we would fix and update that unit prior to releasing. Over time, we would update the entire building and increase the rents with each newly renovated apartment.

We've also had projects where the buildings were fairly stable, and we were just trying to optimize performance. Construction and upgrading were not required but we did work to manage the expenses and collections. Our intent was to make these properties run as efficiently as possible.

All the buildings we have purchased and managed have been very successful and, in most cases, have performed better than the properties around us. This shows that we can outperform the market. (Of course, another part of this is buying the correct building in the first place which you can read about in our book *FINDING AND FINANCING APARTMENT BUILDINGS: Proven Ways to Get it done*.)

Over the years we have grown from a couple of small buildings to a relatively large portfolio. We now have both a property manager and a maintenance manager who take care of most of the day to day management needs. Both managers report directly to us. So, while we have less day to day interaction with the residents, we are still very involved in the operations and management of our apartments.

We also have additional resources for areas that need more expertise. For example, we have several attorneys for different purposes. One helps us with real estate purchasing. Another one deals with landlord-tenant law and works with our insurance companies on coverages and policies. Our resources, education and experience have come together to build the operation that we have today, but it is all based on our original hands-on efforts.

Our goal has always been to buy buildings where we can use our skills to improve either the ongoing revenue or overall property value or both. Because of this, we have seen the extremes from high to low management and upgrade needs.

Knowing what we know now is why we are so passionate about teaching others. Going into apartment investing with some guidance and help can turn a bad situation into something manageable or even positive. We hope that by reading this, and our other books, you will be better prepared to take the leap into larger buildings with the confidence and knowledge to be successful and enhance your life.

Screen Your Applicants

Screening Criteria

A big mistake many apartment investors make is not adequately screening applicants when they come in the door. It's so easy to do - or not do in this case. There are many people that make this mistake, especially when they are small companies and/or just starting out. They feel they don't have access to the resources to verify incomes and do full background and credit checks. They assume that if the person looks reasonable, says they have a good job and pays the application fee, well, how bad could it be? There are so many things that can slip through the cracks if you're not doing adequate screening.

Screening is the bare minimum. If you aren't checking on who you're allowing into your building, you could be causing yourself a lot of pain and cost down the road. This is because once they get in, it is awfully hard to get them out. If you've made a mistake and accepted the wrong person, you have a real problem because they now have a lease. They have a contract and the right to stay there.

In addition, while they are living in your building, they could be driving your good tenants out. If they have a lot of visitors, parties at night, or general disruptive behavior, then the good people who are living in your building will want to get away as soon as possible. They may be requesting to break their lease, or not renew when the time comes. The disruptive people will cause damage to the entire building not just to the unit they rent. They will drive out good people and give your building a bad reputation.

The reason that so many new landlords skip the upfront screening is because of a perceived lack of resources and maybe a desire to not spend money to hire it out. There have been a lot of law changes in the last five or 10 years around fair credit and fair housing. These changes relate to what you can and can't exclude, what you can and can't check for and with the fair credit, it's become tougher to get credit reports and information from applicants online. The good news is, there are screening companies out there. So, even if you're a smaller investor, you can and should hire a screening company.

You can send an application to a screening company and give them your criteria. They have the connections to pull credit reports and do criminal background checks. They can also call and do income and/or job verifications, call prior landlords and do rental verifications. These are all the things you should be going through. You need to be sure your future tenants have the income to pay the rent once they move in and have a stable job history so they can continue to pay.

We require our applicants to have three and a half times rent as their income. The rent is our threshold, so regardless of what the rent amount is, the gross income they must make is three and a half times that rent. That criteria balances out whether it's a higher or lower end building. Our requirement is not a certain dollar amount of earnings. It is three and a half times the rent for the unit they want to occupy.

Right now, in Missouri, a landlord is legally able to require a level of income for an apartment. Check with your landlord-tenant law attorney to verify that this is still legal in your area. This is all bound by Fair Housing as far as the rules you can and can't use to screen people but as of right now, income can be a requirement. You do have to consider all aspects of income like a pension, social security, disability, some sort of housing assistance voucher, etc. You can't exclude based on the type of income. Basically, you can't say, "Oh, you have to have a certain type of job to rend from us". As of right now, you can still say "we need the total collected income between all your various source of income to meet a certain threshold."

Therefore, get the background check and verify the applicant has the required income to meet the needs of the rent.

On a side note you may be wondering why we require 3.5x rent for the income. That is because of the other costs of life. When they move in, they will still have a cell phone bill, food, recreation, and now they will have an electric bill, gas bill, cable bill or any other utilities they may need to pay associated with the unit.

We want to make sure they the applicant can afford to move into the unit and continue to pay for the other items in their life. If you move someone in with 100% of their income needed for rent then, when they have to choose between paying rent or eating, they will most likely chose paying for food. This will lead to a bad situation if not immediately, then somewhere down the line. It is better to know this up front and do your best to only move people in who can afford to live there.

Let's go through other screening criteria. You need to be checking on income as mentioned above. Next, you need to be doing a criminal background check, however, you need to consult with your attorney to be sure about what you legally can and can't screen for.

Felonies as a blanket statement aren't allowed anymore as a means for disallowing residence. To understand this, you must realizethat not every felony is created equal. A felony that involves anything like an assault or burglary where there could be a risk to the property you're managing or the fellow residents at the property would qualify. A felony due to drug possession might not fall into the same realm as one could say, "Well, it is not really dangerous to the property if this person happened to get caught one time with a minimal amount of pot."

It is violent crime or a chronic history of crime that would be a problem or risk to the building and residents. However, as always, check with your attorney.

So, once you have checked the income and background you will then need to check the applicant's credit. We are less concerned about specific credit scores. Sometimes people fresh out of school or fresh out of college might not have much credit built up. A lot of people end up making mistakes and getting some bad credit scores. What we really look for is if they are paying their bills and keeping up with their utility accounts. Have they paid all that was owed to their prior landlords and have they ever had any prior collections or judgments against them? These are all indicators that they may not pay their bills in the future.

The next step is to check their rental history. For most people, if they rented in the past, they should be able to provide prior landlords as references. Call the prior landlords to see if the applicant left with any damages. Did they cause any problems or disturbances to their neighbors? Were there any noise complaints about them? You generally want to get an idea if they're going to take care of the property and keep it in good condition and if they might cause disruptions with the neighbors and the neighboring properties or neighboring residences.

If you fail to screen, or don't complete a full screening, there is a chance that you could move in bad tenants. A lot of people probably aren't going to cause a problem, but some people will. Troublesome tenants may apply, put down an application, fill out all the information and pay for the application We've had people that have applied for apartments, that have told us flat out, "I've never had an eviction, this isn't going to be a problem." Or they will say, "I always pay my rent on time" and then we do a background check and find out they are in the middle of an eviction right now. People might be dishonest, or they might not really understand the consequences of their actions. Either way, you don't want those people in your building.

The risk that you have if you are moving somebody into your building who has had an eviction, financial problems or has had a previous tendency not to pay their rent, is they now have a habit of making you, the property owner the last person on their list to pay. They're going to pay their cellphone and their cable and everybody else before they pay you. It's an indicator that you are likely to have financial problems with them going forward.

In addition, if someone had a criminal background and they committed a violent crime, assault, burglary or anything like that on your property, you could be liable.

Not knowing someone is a violent criminal is not an adequate excuse. "Oh, I had no idea this person would be violent" is not an adequate defense in court nor to your other residents. A criminal background is something that you need to screen for, so you don't put yourself and your other residents at risk.

Allowing tenants to move in who have not passed the screening can cause you huge problems. Once an undesirable tenant is in, they will have a lease and it is going to be much harder to get them out. There will be difficulties even if you take the legal action of saying, "Look you're in violation of your lease. We are going to terminate your lease and evict you." In some states, that may take up to four or more months! The process of filing, getting a court date, getting eviction judgment, getting everything through, will easily take six weeks in Missouri, which is a more landlord friendly state. That's a long time to have someone in your building who is causing problems.

Do a full background check and reach out to other landlords. If you think the prospective tenant might cause a problem for you, your property or for other residents or neighbors, then don't approve their application.

How to Screen

To do the background screening, you can either hire a professional screening company or you can get software that helps you do it yourself. We have purchased some management software that allows us to do credit and criminal background checks and then we directly check with prior landlords and get income verification.

If you don't have the time, resources or access to do these things yourself, hire a professional screening company. Provide them with your criteria and they will gather the information and give you a report. They might even be able to give you a recommendation. They can basically say, "All right, based on the background of this person and the criteria you gave us, we recommend or do not recommend this person as a tenant."

Where to Start

To keep from getting into these problems, the first thing to do is define clear criteria. These help you understand what you are looking for and gives you information to share with your applicants. You want to let your applicants know what you will be checking and that it will actually be done.

This is important for several reasons. If the applicant believes that you will check (which you will) and they know they won't pass, they may withdraw their application right away. This saves you the time and expense of doing the check.

It is also important because as the landlord you must be consistent. You can't accept one person with a certain background and deny another person in with the exact same background. You are now subject to a fair housing discrimination, "Well, why did you let one person move in with an eviction and this person not move in with eviction." If they both have evictions, you need to treat them the same. There are some criteria you can add like, "if the eviction was more than 5 years ago it doesn't matter" but whatever your criteria you must know it, understand it and apply it equally to all. If you're consistent and clear, then you're much more likely to be protected from any sort of discrimination claim or suit.

Once you have your criteria, then figure out how you're going to do the screening. You can go through a third party or do it yourself, but you must start doing this right away. You need to determine: "This is our policy. These are our criteria, and this is how we're going to send this information to the screening company." Knowing these things means when you get an application, you know exactly what to do. You don't want your or your team to be thinking, "Boy, I don't know where to send this thing." If that is the case, then you will most likely not follow through and complete the screening.

We have a friend who is a good example of the need to be consistent and especially establish and explain the screening rules up front. Our friend did do screenings, but he didn't explain the process upfront to folks nor did he gather enough information from the applicant.

He had a woman with two children apply for a one-bedroom apartment. Our city's occupancy permits require three people to live in at least a two-bedroom apartment. He had no control over this law, and it is the same for everyone within the city. After running his background check, he denied her because of the occupancy issue. Well, she sued him, saying that he denied her for reasons based on race. His insurance company decided it was easier to pay than fight, so they just paid her off. He ended up getting a new insurance agency and having a lot of issues because he didn't realize she had two children and explain the criteria for apartment size up front.

If he would have just gotten all of her information at the beginning; "How many people are moving in? Oh, I don't have any two bedrooms available." before he even began the process, he would have saved himself a lot of time and trouble. Even if they are city requirements, the applicant may not be aware that she needs to be looking for a two-bedroom unit. This is just one illustration of the need to make all expectations and requirements clear to everyone up front.

Why Screening is Imperative

It is sometimes difficult to hold to the criteria and complete the screening process. It is easy to get anxious to fill an apartment. Imagine you've had this one apartment that you spent a lot of time and energy renovating and it's beautiful and it's ready to go but, you're just not finding anybody to move in. Then, somebody comes along that wants to move in right now. "Oh man, I need to move in tomorrow. I'm in a hurry. I've got the first month's rent, security deposit, last month's rent. I'll even prepay three month's rent if I can move in today. I understand this is not normal but ..." They always have a very good story.

They may get you with, "The screening is going to take three to four days! I don't have that much time. I just moved. My house had a fire." There are a lot of stories, and this happens often. You need to stay consistent, so you don't get caught up in, "Boy, I'm anxious to have somebody in there now." We have done that a few times and it was always a mistake. We got an applicant that we thought. "Okay, this seems pretty reasonable. I'll run the application later. We'll give them the keys now. They gave us the money, we signed the lease, everything will be fine." Not a single time that we've done that have we thought, "Wow, that was a great idea." or "that really worked out well for us."

Usually that prepaid rent that they promised is a little bit short, "Oh well, you know, I started to prepay three months, but I only have the two months on me. I'll get to the third month, next week," and the next thing you know that's the last payment you'll received from them. It's a risk, especially for small investors when you're first start off and you don't have a management system and you don't have a management company. It's very easy to get sucked into, "Boy, I really want to rent this today and I hate to see this applicant go somewhere else" but you must remind yourself to stay consistent and follow the process.

Faster, Easier and More Efficient Screening

You also need to get the background check done quickly. This means either using a screening company or management software that has quick access to things like background checks.

The world is moving very fast and most applicants will not wait three or four days for you to run an application. When they're out looking for an apartment, they're looking for an apartment today or this weekend. They're putting in applications at two or three different places and the first one that calls them back will get their business. They are not going to say, "Well, no. I want to wait until Joe calls me back to find out if I was approved over there."

Up until they have made a commitment, applicants will continue to look. While they are waiting for you, it is likely they will get anxious and think, "Well, if he can't approve me in three or four days, he's probably not going to approve me" and they'll move on. You must find a way to get the accurate background and screening information as quickly as you can.

Repairs, Repairs, Repairs

The best way ensure failure in apartment investing is to cut back on your maintenance. We have seen this happen a lot when people get into tight financial straits and think they need to save money. "Boy, we've got a couple of bills coming up, insurance is due, the taxes are due, I had two people move out." When money gets tight like this they think, "Well, I just won't fix whatever is broken next month or I won't fix it this summer. I'll band-aid it and put it back together and it will be fine." At the time it seems like a small delay but those minor repairs can become major repairs very quickly.

Maybe, if you have several empty units or money is a little tight, you decide to skimp a little on the upgrades to one of your units. Maybe you skip the new stove or whatever, making that unit less desirable. You might think that just for that one unit, "I'll discount the rent slightly. I know it seems a little older, so I'll just knock a little off the rent." This is a very slippery slope. Once you start it is easy to discount more and more rents and now you are collecting less and less even as you rent your units.

In addition, usually those "band-aid" fixes will come back to haunt you. They will pop up again, becoming more and more expensive each time until the only solution is a major repair. If this is a large cost, it may be too much, so you don't fix it and that unit becomes un-rentable. As soon as you reach that level, it is a downward spiral. This is a thing that happens very quickly and is the cause of many foreclosures or even vacant or abandoned buildings.

You say, "How in the world does someone who has all these apartments end up having something totally empty. You just keep it filled and you'll be fine." Well, it all starts when you cut back on maintenance. It may be a big enough issue that you can't get an occupancy certificate but even if it is smaller, it may prevent quality tenants from signing a lease. Every month a unit is empty is rent you cannot recover.

It also takes so much more time to be dealing with small repairs constantly. Some of these repairs like furnaces or AC units may require immediate fixing for safety reasons and now you and/or your maintenance people are bouncing all over the place trying to keep things together and running. Your tenants are not happy. They don't want to renew next year, and they move out.

You'd be amazed at how quickly a well-run building can spiral out of control when you start cutting back on needed repairs and maintenance. Do not let yourself get caught in this downward spiral.

The Common Temptation to Skip Repairs

You may wonder why cutting back on maintenance is such a common mistake. Probably because they think that they're saving money. That, however, is short term thinking and will not serve you as an investor.

It is much better to put in something new than to fix an older item multiple times. In the Saint Louis area, a good example is air conditioners. If you have a small leak in a cooling line or the condenser, it might be tempting just to patch the line, recharge it and try to get through the year. You might be thinking "I could have replaced it for $2,000 but I can refill it for $200."

You refill it three or four times, you're now in $800 and it's still, $2,000 to replace it. You are spending more over the lifetime of the unit than you would have if you just replaced it at the beginning. People get caught in this mindset of, "Well, I'll save the money now so that makes it okay." You need to think long term and consider the lifetime cost (money, time, ease of renting, etc.) of what you are doing.

You may think a unit is a little dated but, "Is it really worth spending the time and money to update?" This upgrade might be the difference between getting a higher rent and leasing it right away or having it empty and leasing at a lower rate. It's a trap of trying to save for the short term but you end up losing in the long term.

Think of it as an investment. Buying the apartment building was an investment, but that mindset should not stop after buying. You need to remember that every time you do work on the building you are investing in your long-term earnings and the value of the property. Rather than just pocketing the rent proceeds and not fixing anything, think, "I'm going to invest it back by replacing the air conditioners or fixing the kitchens or in this one particular unit, I'm going to invest by putting new flooring in the kitchen."

The pay-back of putting a new countertop in the kitchen is going to be better than the savings of not doing it. "I'm going to be able to push the rent up $25 to $30 a month, so my investment is paying me back." You need to look at it as an overall investment strategy, not just how much you are saving.

The biggest consequence of cutting back on maintenance and repairs, and we keep using the same term, is a downward spiral. An extreme example is a property that we actually bought from someone who got stuck in this trap. They kept cutting corners on repair costs and possibly they did not have or hire the right maintenance team. Things weren't getting repaired. Things weren't getting replaced. The next thing you know they would start saying, "Well, we're running a little tight on money. The stove went out over here. I've got an empty apartment over there. I'll take the stove out of that apartment to fill this apartment, so I don't have to pay for a new stove."

They saved some money by not paying for the new stove but now the empty apartment doesn't have a stove, so it is not rentable. Then, the next stove that dies you take that from a different apartment, continuing in the same way with the furnace or an air conditioner. "Well, the air conditioner went out, but the apartment is empty, I'll fix it at the end of summer, so I don't have to write the check for that right now." Now you're waiting all summer and the apartment is empty.

You're not filling your vacant apartments so you're not getting the rents. Then suddenly you realized that you're falling behind on the amount of rent you are collecting. You are not even collecting enough to pay the mandatory bills. Now, you get desperate and you fall into the first mistake. You start moving people in without screening them. You start moving people in that don't meet your criteria. "They don't really meet my criteria, but they've got the cash in hand and I really need that rent check today so, okay, I'll let you move in. Give me the rent check. Great! Now I've got that in my pocket. Oh dear, it turns out I'm not going to collect anymore rent from you."

"Now, I've got to evict you and I am actually incurring more costs. I got one month's rent and maybe a security deposit, but now, I'm spending all that money to get you to move out and I'm losing the opportunity to have someone in the apartment who will pay me."

This building was across the street from one of our buildings. It was 24 units and by the time he finally gave up the building, only six of the units were even occupiable. The rest of them had been scavenged to try to keep the rest of the units running. He was running out of money and it eventually got so far out of hand that he drove the building into the ground.

He ended up not being able to pay his mortgage. The bank took it back and he lost that entire investment. This is a sad tale, but it points out that you really must look at your investing strategy. It's not just about saving money. I'm not saying waste money, but you have to consider if what you are going to do is a smart investment. "Do I need to invest in this air conditioner? Do I need to invest in this kitchen so that I get the payback of keeping this unit rented and occupied to give me the value and return that I need from my property?"

Getting and Keeping on Top of Maintenance

How do you get on top of the maintenance problem? The first thing is to do an audit of your maintenance issues. Evaluate where you are you spending time and money on maintenance. Along with major concerns, look for things that are relatively inexpensive, but they continuously turn up as something to fix. You should be able to find these by looking at your expense records.

Next do a physical inspection of your properties. Go through occupied and non-occupied units and really assess their current condition. Are you on the verge of a lot of failures? Create a list of all the issues you're facing and then, prioritize your biggest payback.

If you have a vacant unit that has not been rentable because it needed something, maybe that's the first place to start. Get that one fixed up so you can get it occupied and restart the cash flow on that unit. Once that is going, now you've got some extra cash flow you can use to address the next issue. Maybe it's a unit that is occupied but the resident has been in there a long time. That unit is at a discounted rent because you have not updated it, so the condition is getting older and you haven't done any rent increases. Could you go in there, do a few repairs, maybe clean the place up, and get a rent increase out of the current resident in exchange for the update?

You don't even have to have turnover and now, the next thing you know, you have more cash flow again. Plus, the resident may be happier and locked in to stay with you long term. You really have to go through the units to identify and create a list of all of your opportunities. List the things you need to address and then prioritize them. Look for "Where am I going to start? Where is the biggest bang for my buck?" Start with where you can have the biggest impact and then work your way down.

Maintenance Audit Details

It is really important to do regular maintenance audits. We go through common areas and exteriors about once a month. The common areas I'm referring to include the basement, hallways, stairwells and exteriors.

Walk around the building. We check the outside to make sure we don't have any cracked windows or screens that are broken or missing. Once one of our trees was growing into the side of the building. The tree was scratching the building and the gutters, so we knew it needed fixing. Also, we realized that the gutter was overflowing when it rained. These are things you need to look for. Check to see if the outside lights are working. Are the hallway lights working? What about in the basement? Is everything clean and tidy? Do you see any leaks or plumbing issues?

Then, quarterly or every six months, it depends on the property, we do go through each unit and do complete a walk-through inspection. (We do mean each unit.) We check the vanities but one of the biggest things we check is the plumbing. Are there any leaks, especially under the sinks or around the toilets? We make sure we don't see any broken windows or damaged doors. We want to be sure there is nothing that's going to cause further damage if it isn't repaired. Plumbing is the biggest potential problem.

Also look up. Is there any evidence of roof damage or leaks that might not have been reported? Any issues with the roof can become extensive and expensive and may cause damage to the building itself. A roof leak may damage the drywall or plaster. It may even start damaging the wood, including the joists and the framing. If you miss this or let it slide, what could have been a small patch on the roof for a few hundred dollars can become a much more expensive fix of the very framework of the building.

Another mistake that investors make is seeing the best value for investment as a newly built building. Some investors may even skimp on repairs on a building they already own so they can save money to buy the new building. Really, however, spending on maintenance for the current building is an investment in and of itself.

They might think, "I can do these other repairs again after I get the money from the next building." That is just an incredibly short sided and dangerous move. Your cash, especially if you used it all, has been sucked away in this new acquisition Now, what happens if you do have an air conditioner that completely goes out in the middle of July when it's 110. That resident is not going to stay there and legally they would have the right to say, "This is not an occupiable apartment when it is 110 degrees without functioning air conditioning, I've got the right to move out because you're not fixing it and keeping it habitable for me." The same problem would come up if you had a sewer issue or any sort of major catastrophe.

If you don't have the money to repair your first building, you're going to potentially risk losing those residents. So, even though you might think adding a newly built building with a higher return would be a good thing to do, it may not actually be the best move. If you really view it as these repairs are an investment in increasing your rents, your returns and your occupancies, that's huge.

This was an entire strategy around one of the apartment buildings we recently purchased. System-wise, it was in pretty good shape, but it was a little bit dated. Things were older, and interiors hadn't been updated. Some of the air conditioners had limped along for a long time.

We really didn't do much massive capital improvement, we just kept reinvesting in better maintenance. We fixed issues as they came up. When an air conditioner would have an issue, we just completely replaced it, because we didn't want to keep fighting it. Through upgrading services like air conditioning, and interiors, we were able to increase rents and occupancy. The gross rent on that building has increased well over 20% just through doing more proactive maintenance and strategizing our maintenance around what's the highest return for dollars spent.

If the person moves out, do you do a significant upgrade or you say, "Well, I don't have the money so I'm just going to leave it a little dated the way it is."?

We chose to invest in doing some upgrades and got the paybacks through higher rents, but we did not go through the whole building all at once. It's been 18 months and we have just been gradually updating and fixing it. It's gotten us massive returns and a whole lot less stress. It isn't exactly a whole new building, but it did increase returns by 20%.

During those 18 months, we took a bit of a hit on our cash flow because we were reinvesting in the building. However, after the 18 months, we had options as to what to do with the building, since it was doing so much better. We could refinance it, consider selling it, or there were even other exit strategies. These options gave us a very large bang for our buck within 18 months, which is a great turnaround time for a property. We did this without having the additional stress of managing and spreading our money between two buildings.

We didn't have to say, "Okay well, let me pick or choose" instead we could say, "This is the building. Let me get this up and running, increasing this building's cash flow and then have choices as to where to go next."

We have a rule here that each building should pay for itself. There has been a time or two, especially at the start with a brand-new building, when that might not have been true. Normally, however, we look at each investment as a single unit and say, "This investment needs to be able to stand on its own two feet. We don't rob Peter to pay Paul."

Maintenance is an Investment

To successfully invest in an apartment building prioritize your maintenance. Carefully evaluate where you can get the highest return for your money and start with those repairs. Then continue to work through all the issues in order of importance. As long as you think of maintenance as an investment, you should be fine. Your spending will keep the building running, functional and profitable. If you start cutting corners, then you're cutting off the legs of your own investment.

Faster, Easier and More Efficient Repairs and Maintenance

To get results faster, easier and more efficiently, hire professionals. This is very important! Even when, as an apartment investor, you are self-managing, you need to hire some professionals. It is difficult to prioritize maintenance spending if you don't know how much various needs will cost. Bring in a professional to get an estimate. Get bids on projects you're going to start soon. That will help you decide, "Yes, this is where spending this dollar amount is the best to get me this amount of return," Getting advice and information from professionals, plus even having them do the work, will help improve your management.

In addition, work that is well done by a professional will be less likely to come up again as a problem. If you've used a professional, then you can feel confident when they fix it, that it's fixed permanently.

 Also, as you use professionals, you can get warranties and build relationships. If anything goes wrong, you know who to contact. If they replace an AC unit and they do something wrong or the fix has a problem, they usually guaranty the work up to a certain point. This is especially true if you plan to grow. They are more likely to fix it when they know that 40 or 60 or 100 units are in the balance. With that potential future business, they want to keep you happy, and they can see that you will grow because you are keeping your units well-functioning, neat, and maintained.

When "Good Intentions" Doom You

Good intentions can sometimes lead to problems. This can be especially true with rent collections. Many times, particularly newer apartment investors, might not realize it is critical to make collecting rent on time a top priority. Sometimes people think they're doing the right thing by letting the rent date slide because "the renter probably has a problem or issue." The investor might feel, "I'm helping them out so I'm going to give them a little more time." This is very dangerous, especially if you think of this property as your investment.

If this is an investment, which it is, then you cannot allow people to live there for free. It's nothing against them personally but, by not paying they are stealing a collectible rent that you could get from somebody who could afford the apartment. You must manage those collections. What feels like, "Oh well, I'll be generous this one time," can suddenly and quickly escalate to - by the end of the month, then into next month, and finally not at all. If you don't manage it at the front end you might not notice they have not paid until near the end of the month and now you are on a downward track.

You realize, "Oh man. What happened?" They said, "I can get this to you next week." Well, next week is already next month and by the time you roll over into the first of the next month, they are two months behind. If they can't pay one month in one month, it is unlikely they can pay two months in one month. Now they are really behind, and you are chasing them to get two month's rent. Suddenly you are in the midst of an ugly process. Even if you come up with a plan, now you must manage that payment plan.

Are you going to remember they are supposed to give you $200 this week and $200 next week? It's a dangerous spiral and it can happen very quickly, if you don't carefully manage your collections every month. As you grow and get more apartments, it can become even harder to keep track of everything. "Well, we got a bunch of rent checks. I haven't really looked at our delinquency list. It feels alright so we must be doing OK." That's totally different than actively managing your collections.

Why People Make this Mistake

Probably the main reason people have trouble managing their collections is fear of confrontation. Some people really don't like making that phone call saying, "Hey, I haven't received your payment. If you don't either pay or move out, it's going to become a legal issue." Some people are just not comfortable having that conversation. "Well, I feel bad if they say they can't afford to pay. I feel I should help if they say they're working on it and will have it by a certain time."

They avoid the confrontation issue, until it becomes such a large dollar amount that, "Oh dear, now I have to address it." Unfortunately, now you are addressing it from a point of frustration. I've seen some people that wait until three month's rent are due, before they're start following up. Now, they're frustrated and they're desperate. "I have to have it right now." That's not a proactive way to deal with it. You need to deal with it early in the first month.

They're trying to avoid the uncomfortable conversation and the confrontation. Unfortunately, it is going to come. Whether it comes today, or in a week, or two weeks, or a month, it is going to come. You need to practice being proactive and addressing it right away.

The Consequences of this Mistake

Keep in mind every apartment only has 12 months of potential rent each year. That is all you can ever collect. You can't collect 13, you can't collect 15. All you can collect is the 12 months each year. If someone doesn't pay for just one month, you have lost one-twelfth of that unit's ability to collect rent for the year. That is a loss of eight and a half percent of your annual gross income from that apartment due to one month of uncollected rent. One unit in a large building may not feel like much, but it can add up quickly.

The consequences are losing out on your revenue. If you're not addressing it proactively, it can become two months before you know it. By the time it gets to that point, you're starting to run out of options for motivating the tenant to move. Early in the process you can use their security deposit to cover your losses. You can tell them, "Well, if you can't pay, just move out. We can use your security deposit to cover what you owe. There might even be some left over for us to return. We can just terminate the lease and part ways."

If you let the person get two or three months behind, the security deposit is not going to make you whole. You can't offer to let them move and part ways. Now you must file an eviction which means paying attorney costs and court fees.

In addition, the resident is probably going to stay in your apartment through the entire court process. Early in the process, you can offer to let them move out instead of getting an eviction on their record but once you filed the eviction, you've lost that bargaining chip.

Now, you're negotiating from a point of weakness. It just went from maybe costing you one month's worth of rent to costing you three months' worth of rent, plus an attorney and court costs. It is also likely they will not do a good job of cleaning the apartment and may even cause damage. Therefore, the costs to make the apartment ready for the next tenant are likely to go up as well. Suddenly this one residence that was slightly behind, can end up costing thousands of dollars.

There are also consequences to the building if you are not collecting all your rents. The rents pay for building maintenance and upgrades so your lower income can cause problems for the entire property. If you have people that can't afford to live there, you do not want them in your buildings. Take care of this problem right away.

What You Should Do Instead

To get ahead of the problem, be proactive. Make sure that your lease is clear about the consequences for not paying the rent. Make sure it states that the rent is due on the first of every month. Have late fees that will be applied by the 5th of the month. If the late fees don't kick in until the 10th or the 15, you're going to have a tough time supporting the argument that, "Hey, we've got to have this rent at the beginning of the month to make sure we have the cash in the accounts to cover that month's bills."

Any time you give them for paying past the 1st, is basically free financing for them. Make sure that there is a late fee if they don't pay at the beginning of the month. Late fees are there as an incentive to pay rent on time to avoid getting the late fee. If you state late fees will apply on the 5th then apply that fairly to all and hold to it. Also include in your lease when you will file for evictions. You want to make sure there are no surprises with a tenant who isn't paying their rent on time.

You also must have a process for giving residents a pay or quit notice. This is the notice that says, "This is your legal notice that you need to pay the rent or quit your possession of the premises and return it back to me. If you fail to do either one of those things, I'm left with no other option than eviction." If you do this earlier in the month you could negotiate terms with the tenant. "I understand you've lost your job. I understand that's really tough, but you can't afford to stay there. We can't afford to have you staying here for free. "

Talk to the tenant. "If you move out, turn back over the apartment, turn in your key and leave the place clean, it will be better for both of us. We'll apply your security deposit to your outstanding charges and if you move out quick enough there might even be a little bit left on your deposit that we can give back to you." You can negotiate that. If it's already the end of the month, there is no prorated rent left to give back. There is no way they're going to be able to get out in time to even have that as an option. The sooner you address the problem, the sooner you will know the situation. "Oh dear, they just said they lost their job. They're not going to be able to come back from that," versus, "I addressed that on the first. They said their company messed up their payroll."

Or you may hear that they're going to pay it on the 7th and they understand that we'll add a late fee to anything after the 5th. So then, you're also setting the precedent for future months, "Oh man, I know I don't want to get it in late because even though I had a good excuse, I still had to pay the late fee." That way you're also not setting that precedent of, "Well, this time I avoided the late fee," telling them the late fee has no effect if they have a good enough story.

What to Do If You Made This Mistake

To fix this problem if you already have it, start today! Address the issues that you've been ignoring. Plus, if you've been ignoring this, it probably means you've been ignoring other issues as well. A confrontation will be a negative thing. You might think, "Oh man, I've already got three people that are really past due." Unfortunately, no matter how long you put it off, it isn't going to get better We've always found that anytime we avoided a difficult conversation, and sometimes it happens unintentionally, that it always gets worse and you still must deal with it.

There were times when we had so much going on between new buildings, new projects and construction updates that we lost track of time and realized, "Oh dear, it's already the 15th or 18th of the month and we haven't done a solid review of our collections for the other properties." You're working from behind the eight ball if you don't address it quickly. We had to jump right in to see if there were any collection or delinquency issues. Although we were a bit late, it was still better than if we had waited until after the first and then realized, "I've got all these people that owe me two month's rent."

How to prevent making this mistake in the future

The best way to keep track of everything is to set up a calendar. Make sure that you know what day of the month rent is due which, by the way, should always be on the first. What day of the month do you assign late fees? What day of the month do you start contacting people and how do you contact them? Do you want to set up an email reminder? Are you able to do text reminders? Do you call them? At what point do you give them notices? Do you use a paper or electronic pay or quit notice? Make sure there is a monthly calendar defining when you take each of the various steps and how you plan to take them.

It is a reality that sometimes your renters run into financial difficulties. That is a difficult situation, but you must make sure they are prioritizing you when deciding which bills to pay first. You do not want them to prioritize the cellphone, cable or various other things over their rent. You make sure you are first by adding late fees, following up and calling them. If they choose to prioritize others over you it is probably because those guys are aggressively calling them, and you are not.

They may think, "I can put off my management company or my landlord for a bit because they haven't really bothered me yet." By the time you do bother them, they've spent all their money paying off the other bills. There is nothing left to pay you until the next check which will be two more weeks down the road even if they found a new job.

If they are in a truly difficult situation, you certainly can work with people to set up payment plans. You must, however, make sure it is an adequate plan, that gets them caught up in a reasonable amount of time. Then, you must enforce that plan rigorously.

Okay, you may not want to file the eviction. You feel you can work it out with them, which is fine, but you must document your plan. Write it down, set the due dates and if they miss those due dates, you must proceed with legal action.

Fast, Easy and Efficient Rent Collections

Having a good tracking system for your collections is very important. If you're using accounting software like QuickBooks, make sure you find a report you can run that shows outstanding invoices or uncollected rents plus whatever other information you may want to review.

If you use management software, it should have a delinquency report. You can run the report and it will show you every single person that has any sort of balance due, from 50 cents all the way up to however many months they may be behind. You can manage from that report but must also manage your calendar, so you know when you're going to look at your report and what you're going to check.

You can also do it manually, although, not many people keep a ledger anymore. Most likely you would use a spreadsheet like Excel. Whatever you're using to keep track of your apartment finances, it must be easy see the rents that are due and those that have been paid, along with the dates.

Make sure you review this list in a timely manner and on a set schedule. It doesn't need to be every day as it can consume your life, especially if you are dealing with properties that are in lower income areas where there are a lot of collection challenges. It is important, however, even with other priorities, to make sure that you review your collections on a consistent and regular schedule.

Other Profit Boosts

Of course, you need to manage your overall revenue and that encompasses multiple factors. A big part of that is managing your collections which we have already discussed, making sure you are collecting rent from all the apartments you have leased. There are, however, many other things that contribute to revenue which include turnovers, vacancy rates, downtime and rent levels.

Are you managing how long it takes between someone moving out and a new tenant moving in? Remember, every unit only has 12 months of potential rent that you can collect. Every time you lose a month, you've lost one-twelfth of that entire year's rent for that unit. If it normally takes a month to turn a unit around and re-rent it, you should evaluate what can be done to reduce that time. Some units may take more work than others but have a goal for your turnaround time. We target for two weeks or less to go from one tenant moved out to the unit ready to show and have someone move in. If you can reduce the turnaround time you can make a significant increase in your overall rent collection.

Another aspect of revenue is to manage the level of your current rents. This includes both market rates for newly available units and your existing rent rates. When people are coming up for renewals, are rent costs for that market moving up? Are you looking at doing rent increases? Do you need to make concessions? Can you raise prices when you're marketing your apartments? On the other hand, sometimes you need to lower prices to make sure a new person moves in and it stays occupied? You want to manage that revenue.

It's not always about getting the top dollar rent. For example, let's say you had $600 apartment and you wanted to see if you can get $700 per month for that apartment. Well if it took you a month to get that $700, you made a hundred for 11 months, so you've made $1,100 but you lost $600 to do it. Maybe that's worthwhile. But what if it takes you two months to fill it. Well now you've made 1,100 but you lost 1,200 so now you've come up too high. It's not always necessarily chasing that highest dollar.

Months Vacant	Months Rented	Monthly Rent	Total Collected
0	12	$600	$7,200
1	11	$700	$7,700
2	10	$700	$7,000
3	9	$800	$7,200

As you can see sometimes getting something rented at a slightly lower monthly rent can be equal to or better than getting the top dollar. Plus, if you were sitting on a vacant unit for 3 months you may feel like you need to drop the price to get someone in, and then you have lost even more. You should make sure to conduct an analysis at least quarterly to determine the various rents of current tenants and market rates for similar apartments, to make sure that you are not falling into the 'top dollar' trap.

It is a balance of getting the appropriate amount of rent but filling the unit quickly, so you don't have vacancy issues. You need to manage your overall revenue including not just the income, but also collections, vacancies, turnover and price points on your renewals.

Managing Apartment Buildings - Time Management

Managing your time is key to successful apartment investing and a happier life.

Where we see many people waste time is firefighting, and we don't mean literally going out and fighting fires. That's a phrase we use when you are jumping from one immediate task to the next, and then to the next focusing on what is urgent but not on what is important. You must to learn how to manage your time and be proactive with collections, maintenance and screening. If you don't manage your time, you're going to find that this building will manage you quickly. You've must get in front of it.

Know your priorities. Know where your maintenance team is spending their time. Know where you're scheduling showings for that day. Try to group things together. If you're doing showings at several different buildings and you need to physically drive to each of them, make sure you schedule the appointments back to back so you're not driving back and forth. Really consider where you are spending your time. Otherwise, if you are not careful, you'll find you have spent an entire week and you have no idea what you actually accomplished.

There are many tools to help with time management. 'A time logger' is a useful phone application. This helps track how much time is spent on various tasks. There are some tasks that you want to make sure you spend enough time on, and there are other tasks where you want to limit your time. A time tracker provides graphs and data to help determine where your is being spent. It was a bit difficult to get used to updating the application each time we changed tasks, but once it became a habit it was much better than pen and paper.

Another helpful hint with time management is to set time limits on certain activities. Work will stretch into the time you give it. If you give yourself a month to complete a report it will take you the whole month. However, if you only give yourself a week, you can get the exact same report completed in that week. Determine specific dates for tasks such as contacting tenants or conducting rent analysis. Then set aside a specific amount of time to complete the task. The first time you do this you may just measure how long it takes you. Then set a goal of reducing the amount of time it takes by 10% the next time you do that task. This will help you ensure that you are setting reasonable goals, but also taking control over your time and your day.

With small investors, one thing that costs some people a lot of time and effort is physically going from property to property. We know some people like small buildings. This is a different investment strategy that will require physically going to multiple buildings for things like maintenance, meeting with a tenant or meeting an applicant. While this strategy can work, you're going to spend a lot of time driving and trying to schedule things because you're not physically in one spot.

We are biased toward a bit larger building, because you can get more economy of scale. Obviously, very large complexes, maximize that, where you've got a clubhouse and a leasing office and other amenities. Not every investor is going to reach that scale.

If, however, you can purchase the majority of your buildings within one area or most of your apartments within one property, you can be much more efficient with your time. You're not going to waste as much time on the road, traveling between appointments, activities and meeting people.

The best way to avoid spending a lot of unnecessary time in your car is to set one day a week to visit your properties. Or, if you are showing the units yourself, make sure to schedule multiple appointments back to back. This will make the trip more worthwhile, and if the applicant doesn't show up it is ok because someone else is coming right behind them.

If you find that most of your day is filled with showings in various locations, you could look at hiring a leasing agent. This person is only working to find you a tenant. They normally collect between ½ to one full month of rent on units where you accept their applicant. You can still do a full background check, and. as long as the leasing agent is clear regarding your approval requirements, then they can inform the applicants. This is a great way to free up your time.

We would, however, recommend you lease a few units yourself before outsourcing. This will help you understand the process and make easier to know when someone is not earning their paycheck. For example, if you were able to rent a unit in 6 weeks and you hire a leasing agent that takes 10 weeks to fill an apartment, that is a problem. They may not be posting as much as you thought they would, or maybe they are not as quick to respond to phone calls as they told you they would be. By knowing the process firsthand, you can better set expectations and know when someone is not living up to their hype.

Finally, if you need even more time back, consider your personal strengths and weaknesses. If there are tasks that you really enjoy doing, or are good and efficient at completing, then keep them. If there are tasks you dread, ones that you avoid every week or month, then find a way to outsource them. In this day and age outsourcing has become easier than ever! There is no reason to keep doing activities that you don't like or are not good at. Depending on the tasks, there are many approaches to outsourcing. It can be a physical person in your area, as in the example of the leasing agent. Or it could be virtual assistant in India, for accounting or posting listing to websites. Find a way to take your time back and control your day. Your family will thank you for being free to spend more time with them.

Marketing Your Property

Be careful that marketing your apartments does not turn into a sinkhole for your time. I've seen owners get really excited about marketing their apartments. They enjoy making sure it's listed everywhere, and it's kind of a fun to get pictures, making sure everything looks sharp with the exact right wording and language in their postings. It's important to market but don't get bogged down with that one thing at the cost of everything else.

Marketing is just one of many tasks to focus on when you're managing an apartment. It is fun to show people pictures of your building, all new and shiny. But this needs to be balanced with managing the tenants, managing the contractors, reviewing your numbers, and looking for new deals. If you are only focused on the marketing you may get a lot of showings, but if the units aren't finished, or the outside doesn't look good, you will not be able to convert them to a paying resident. Don't let yourself fall into the marketing trap. It's an easy thing to do,

As we mentioned before there is much that you can outsource. If you find that you are spending a lot of time on marketing, you may want to consider hiring a leasing agent and having them post to the websites as part of their contract. This will help free up your time to focus on the other areas of your business.

If you love doing the marketing, then maybe consider focusing on that and outsourcing some of the other work. You could even reach out to other building owners and offer to help them with marketing, to help subsidize the expense of outsourcing other tasks.

The point is that there are many different areas of focus that will need your time. There should be a balance between the tasks. No one task should take all your time, leaving the other activities to suffer. It is good to play to your strengths if there is a plan and a process for the remaining items that you are not doing.

Don't Overpay for This

It is easy for apartment investors, especially newer apartment investors, to focus on marketing and advertising and it is easy to overpay for these services. There are many apartment marketing resources that want to charge you, but there are also many free resources that will list and advertise your apartment. As of now Craig's List and Zillow are two very popular free options for anyone to use. Don't get suckered into paying for items that you can get for free.

There are also online tools that share your posts to multiple sites on the internet at no cost to you. You can add pictures and a description, so you really don't have to spend for a high-end premium marketing service.

Rentals are very local game. People are looking for a certain area, a certain location, a certain price point. You don't need national exposure. You don't need to use the number one search result on Google across the country. You should be able to do all the marketing you need for very little or no cost to you.

Technology is always changing and the 'cool' place to search may change, but there are always options. Keep your focus local. Make sure you are in touch with where people in your area look for units and post there. Include enough information so that they can make an informed decision about how suitable your apartment is for them. This includes the monthly rent, utilities that are or are not included, the square footage, and the location. This can save you a lot of unnecessary showings.

Dealing with Tenants

Don't Be an "Ostrich"

Letting bad tenants stay in your apartment building way too long is a classic 'ostrich' mistake that many apartment investors make. That is what we all want to avoid.

Even if you do the screening, even if you do everything else, there will be times when you move someone in that you should not have. This is just a pure numbers game, meaning that statically you are going to get someone moved in that will cause problems. It could be because you didn't catch something on the screening or your tenant allows a boyfriend or girlfriend to move in, or they even just have friends over. Whatever it may be, somebody that is causing problems is now part of your apartment community. They may be disturbing the neighbors, causing noise complaints or not following other rules you laid out when they moved in. A lot of times confronting somebody about rent feels at least like a real business issue. Confronting a bad tenant, can feel more difficult and it is likely that many of you will try to avoid it.

You may think, "Boy, I just hope that guy goes away. Maybe, they'll break up. Maybe it's only this weekend they're going to be loud. I really don't want to say anything because they'll get mad at me and I just don't want to deal with that confrontation." That's where people get stuck wanting to avoid the confrontation. We have seen it. We have seen even seasoned apartment investors not being proactive about having these tough discussions with the disruptive tenants, especially if a building starts to get out of control, However, once you have one disruptive tenant, it's likely that you are going to get two or three bad tenants in the same place. Now the landlord makes an even bigger mistake and starts avoiding the building. They avoid dealing with the situation entirely.

Avoiding these issues is really bad in the long term, even if it's not terrible at the moment. Maybe it is not criminal activity nor is it a safety concern. Maybe someone is just up late making loud noises, playing loud music and disturbing the neighbors. When the neighbor's leases are up, they are not going to renew. They're moving out. They might put up with it until the end of the lease but then they are not coming back. When you go to show that apartment, if people are 'hanging out' and there is loud music, the potential tenants are not going to want to move in there either. So, in order to rent the unit, you may need to lower your criteria or your price or move someone in who was on your 'maybe' list. Otherwise, you may have to keep the unit vacant longer to find a good, highly qualified tenant.

Now, the tenant causing trouble is directly impacting the financials on your property. Even though they seemed like a good choice originally now you realize the mistake. However, if the troublemaker is paying rent on time each month, that can entice an investor to put their blinders on. This is definitely a risk for investors that manage for themselves. It is easy to think, "Well, I have to make sure I get that rent in. I really don't want to say anything to make them angry and have them move out." That's the biggest challenge in apartments. One bad occupant in an apartment can chase-off the entire rest of your building. You would be keeping one unit of rent, but you may lose all or many of the others. That is why it is so important to address bad tenants even if they are paying rent on time.

If it's extreme, they could chase-off the whole building very quickly. You will lose your higher quality tenants that are maintaining the property and keeping it quiet and respectful for their fellow residents. Suddenly you have a problem building. You will still have to move the troublemakers out plus now re-tenant the whole building. It's going to be a nightmare. Crossing your fingers and hoping things will take care of themselves is not the answer and will not work.

There are a few options for you to deal with this issue. If you think that the person you approved moved someone else in, a boyfriend or girlfriend perhaps, then you can address that with the original tenant. Meet with them and let them know (refer to your lease) that every adult that lives on the premises needs to go through the screening process. If they don't want to do it then they can move out and you will not change them an early move out fee.

Also, your lease should include a section regarding respecting their neighbors. If they are playing loud music at night and get police calls, then you can file a disturbance eviction. Before that happens, you can talk to the lessor to remind them of the rules and let them know they are disturbing their neighbors. Normally by the time you know they are already aware that the neighbors are disturbed, but it is good to have the conversation with them anyway.

This issue is one that you will need to pull your head out of the sand and address before you feel the larger pain of having an underperforming or vacant building. Section 1 above has information on taking over your new building and what you should include in your lease agreement.

A Big Fear and How To Deal With It

To review, one of the biggest fears many people have is confrontation and saying the wrong thing. "Boy, I don't want to call somebody and say the wrong thing so now they can sue me or cause trouble in some way." Prepare before you have the conversation. Understand the issue you are calling or meeting about. Know your priorities. What do you want out of the conversation? Think to yourself, "do I need to know the date of payment or the date of move out?" What are you trying to get answered? Just keep to the relevant facts.

You don't want to get caught up in an emotional conversation. Keeping the emotion out of the encounter is very important. Know yourself and play to your strengths. If you are an escalator, meaning you take normal conversations and add drama, then you will need to prepare even more for this step. Getting drawn into an unproductive tangent during the conversation is not going to resolve anything. Keep your eye on what you want to accomplish and do not make it personal or take it personally.

Confrontation is going to happen. If you avoid the situation you get yourself into a downward spiral. Fear comes from people not wanting to do the wrong thing. If you know what you need to talk about, keep the conversation professional, and keep the interaction focused on the issue, then it should be just fine.

The REAL fear should be the bigger problem that will come out of not addressing the situation. If you go into the conversation, knowing what you intend to talk about and knowing your goal, then you are fully prepared to address and confront the issue.

Working with Contractors

We have already discussed dealing with your renters, but another thing that can create a lot of stress and anxiety is dealing with contractors. When dealing with contractors that you have not used in the past, you must get multiple bids and references. This is true whether it is for ongoing maintenance or a one-time job. A lot of times people forget or sometimes are just in a hurry, so they don't ask for and check references. This is a big mistake.

Make sure your contractor is credible because the last thing you want is get partway into a project and be frustrated with their work. If a contractor is doing "shoddy' work or not showing up or being consistent, you're dealing with a big hassle and headache. Now you will need to fire them and find someone else. The project isn't getting done, you're losing time and money, and no one is happy. Make sure before you bring somebody on board as a contractor at your building, that you've done your homework. You know that this contractor is somebody who's credible, will do quality work for a fair price and they can deliver what they're promising.

Having quality workmen who get the work done on time is important to keeping the current tenants happy. If the contractors are taking longer than expected, the existing tenants could get annoyed due to reduced parking, noise before noon, or other complaints. Making sure that you hire someone professional, that can get the job done in an effective and efficient manner is critical.

However, that doesn't mean you need to hire the most expensive contractor that exists in your city. We have worked with many professional people who did a great job for us while keeping our costs in mind.

When we first got into real estate it was during the 2006-2008 boom. This made it very difficult to find good contractors. We hired one contractor who charged by time and materials and seemed very reasonable. Then we performed an audit of their receipts and the biggest cost was going to Home Depot 2-3 times per day. They were not managing their resources or time, and it was costing us money. We addressed this issue with a new edict of no more than one trip to the hardware store per day. His response was that work might have to stop if they didn't have the tools or supplies needed to complete the job. We agreed that was a risk, but that a professional organization should be able to plan 8 hours ahead. We no longer do business with that company.

On the other hand, we met a man while we were doing some construction. He lived a few doors down and stopped by one day to see what was happening. He owned a construction company and gave us his card. This chance meeting has provided almost a decade of positive synergy. He has the same values as we do; honesty, integrity, trustworthiness. We started him on a smaller project and he and his team did a great job. Over the years we have counted on him time and again.

The lesson here is that even if you like who you are working with it never hurts to meet someone new and give them a chance. We now work with many contractors because we have various needs and deadlines. We work with people we like and trust. We have built a reputation around our company and style. Real estate is a small world and you should work to build long-term relationships, so you have connections with the right people and companies.

The Best Tool for Successful Management

We were originally reluctant to get apartment management software, but now can't live without it. The good news is costs have gone way down and it doesn't have to be actual software that is installed. Now you can get a license and download it on your computer. There are so many apps and web-based services that's not terribly expensive, regardless of your size. If you are becoming a larger investor with a big portfolio, you can go with all the bells and whistles. If you're small, there are a lot of apps and websites that can help you as well. The point is, wherever you are, you need some sort of tool to help you keep track of things.

Your software should help you keep track of your maintenance, new resident applications, collections and delinquencies. You need some resource where you can put all information in one place and even if there is a cost, it pays for itself. When we finally migrated from doing QuickBooks and Spreadsheets over to our management software which is an AppFolio software, we were very nervous about the expense. We had a property manager working for us at the time and he was also nervous about the extra time and effort to learn this new system.

Within 90 days, we were both hands down saying, "why in the world didn't we do this a year ago? There is so much time freed up and so much less effort. Things are so much more efficient. We feel less stressed and fewer things are slipping through the cracks."

Again, it doesn't have to be high-end expensive software. Just some sort of tool that helps you keep things together and organized. This is really important.

Some Big Mistakes to Watch Out For

Over Renovating

Many investors like to do renovations. Taking something that is underperforming with the best intentions to make it into a profitable and beautiful building can be fun and exciting. Having a project is also fun. Seeing the change from poorly run to magnificent is very enticing. Many investors think, "I am investing because I want a project, I want to change something". They rush in intending to renovate the whole building. That is a good way to run yourself off the spending cliff.

You may not want to open all the walls on day 1. Once you tear down walls, you are stuck with a major renovation, but you may not be in a position to update 100% of the wiring or plumbing in a building.

In addition, it is easy to over-renovate in apartments. We see that a lot, especially with people that used to do single-family real estate rehabs and flips. They may put granite countertops into a neighborhood that can't support the extra cost. This person may think, "Well I just need $1,000 per month rent to support this. It will be awesome!" But the rent in the neighborhood is only $600 so the unit is over renovated.

The way they understand the world and the way you get the maximum return, is to renovate as much as possible and then sell it for the max profit. In some cases, renovation makes sense, but in other cases it's the smaller stuff that makes sense. It's all about that return on investment. If you want to spend $5,000 improving this apartment but only get an extra $100 worth of rent, it might not be worthwhile. If, however, you spend a thousand dollars on an apartment and get $45 more in rent, well, it's not nearly as updated, but you still got a rent bump.

The rent bump may not big but as a percent you're actually getting a higher return on your investment. Sometimes it is better to spend less and get a smaller rent bump, but you are staying within the rent levels for that area or type of building. Don't just dive in and say, "We need to change everything, we must renovate everything, we are going to gut everything." You can quickly overspend your renovation budget that way.

Start by deciding what spending makes sense and what does not. Understand your numbers. Evaluate how much you should spend, and what you expected to get back in rent. This should help on the front end to determine your budget and how you want to allocate your funds.

Make sure to have a plan before you begin and then stick to that plan as best you can. Surprises are always going to come up. However, if you are staying within your predetermined budget you should be able to handle them better than if you already spent your whole budget without knowing your return.

Ignoring Critical Dates

People forget to plan their month. They blow off critical dates to follow-up with tenants, and just say, "Well, I'm busy, I'll take care of it later, when things come to a head." Instead, you've really got to plan your month out. The way you find the time in your schedule is to do it at the end of the prior month. A lot of your apartment activities, from a deadline standpoint, will happen right around the first of the month. People are moving in, people are moving out, you are collecting rents. You're starting to look at your delinquency rate. Before you get to the last week of the month you should be setting your calendar for the following month. You don't want to wait until the last week because then you probably have move outs, make readies, and other activity already starting. You should focus on getting your calendar set about a week before the end of the month.

About a week before the end of the month, try to sit down and say, "Okay, what are the priorities for next month? Where I can be more proactive than I was this month? How do I make next month better?" Doing that, as you start to make little changes, it snowballs and builds on itself. You'll find that even if you're headed down the wrong path, you can begin moving back in the right direction by saying, "All right, what am I going to do next month that's different?" Then prioritize that and do it.

This monthly reflection can help you stay on track regarding all the items we have discussed. Maybe you think back to a tenant who didn't pay, and you let them slide. Well, you can set a goal for yourself that this month you will address all non-payment within the first 10 days of the month. Then see how you do. What held you back from achieving your goal? This can be used to help you do a better job the following month.

We have tried to follow this advice ourselves. Even though we have a regular agenda, we have calendar reminders for everything. We use Google calendars with appointments on certain days of the month for late fees, for pay-or-quit notices, for eviction filings, for follow-up phone calls, and any other items that are needed for our apartments.

All of this is a process. You are not going to do everything perfectly on day one of buying your first larger building. However, if you keep an open mind and work toward improvement, you can become a successful investor in real estate no matter the market environment.

Our Biggest Mistake and How We Fixed It

Our biggest mistake was not hiring help quickly enough. Alex's background is in engineering. He grew up on a farm. He was used to working with his hands and fixing things himself in order to save a little money. This was a mistake because it limited our ability to grow and it also put quite a strain on our family life. Having a corporate job while actively managing our apartments, doing the maintenance, leasing and everything else was not a good plan. There are only so many hours in the day.

You can't reproduce those hours. You can leverage money and you can leverage a lot of other things for growth. Many times, however, we forget the only way we can leverage time is by hiring people to do things for us. The first step in our recovery was hiring a maintenance crew. Many of those guys are still work for us now. We have had a fantastic relationship. We've built a good rapport. They are guys that we trust. We know we can send them out to a job anywhere and they will knock it out quickly and efficiently. This helped get over that hump of, "Boy, do we really want to have employees working for us?"

We used to have the mindset that, "We have to manage, we have to schedule, and we have to do all that other stuff because it is absolutely important to do and we didn't think anyone else could do it as well as we could." We repeated this same mistake as we kept growing. We hired out maintenance but kept doing all the leasing and all the tenant management ourselves. We just wanted to keep that control. We finally brought in a leasing agent. We went through a couple hiccups and there were a couple of leasing agents that did not work out but when we finally got the right person in place, it was a game changer.

We suddenly had time freed up to focus on the investment, not just focusing on calls and showings and appointments and applications. You need to be aware of your skillsets and your time. Then use that to decide when it makes sense to hire something out. Leverage other people's time to get time back for you. Focus on the highest return for your time and talent.

A Tip If You Are Paralyzed by Fear

If you already own apartments, you may feel you are not in control. It may seem the building is managing you, instead of the other way around. Our advice would be to try some of what we have listed. It doesn't have to be a dramatic change. You can try this out a little at a time. None of the changes suggested in this book are permanent, fixed in stone, or high cost. The best way to break free of some of your fears, is just try a few things at a time.

Make sure you're calling that resident, confronting the expensive contractor who isn't meeting deadlines, reaching out to the leasing agent who isn't bringing in leads. If it is something that you are avoiding, then it is likely the most important thing you need to do.

Is there a resident you have been avoiding? Call them and address the issue. Make sure it's been dealt with. Once you do it a few times, you'll find you get better at it. You'll become good at talking with people about delinquency or whatever other issue. You become more comfortable with addressing problems and having uncomfortable conversations with people.

Being able to address uncomfortable things is an excellent skill to develop so you don't just avoid the problems. Putting your head in the sand doesn't make them go away. The only way to resolve issues is to confront them and deal with them.

The biggest thing to understand when managing apartments is that it is a people business. When you start out, you're managing the residents, contractors, maintenance people, and you might even add lenders and banks. Even when you get to the point of having a leasing agent or property manager, you are now managing those agents. The building is a physical asset that everything is tied to, but almost all your activities will involve working with people. It is very much a people driven business.

One tip that can help immensely, is to write down three things that you really don't want to do. If you find yourself sitting on the couch playing games or not focusing on what needs to be done, write down three things you don't want to do. Then, just pick one of those three and do it. You'll find that it was not as bad and not as scary as you thought it would be.

That trick should help get the ball rolling. "Oh okay. Yes, that phone call, I was really nervous about it, but I made it and it's okay." Now, you can make another phone call and another and then as you get more practice at it, it will naturally be less scary. In our first book _Finding and Financing Apartment Buildings: Proven Ways to Get It Done,_ we describe the need to make 27 phone calls to get our first loan. That was extremely difficult, so we know what you are feeling. Just start with one call.

Final Thoughts On Managing Apartments

In conclusion, our main advice is to as be proactive as you can, because issues aren't going to fix themselves. When it comes to your maintenance, when it comes to addressing tenant issues, when it comes to addressing collections, when it comes to your screening, when it comes to managing your time, when it comes to managing your month, take the time to set up and follow a plan. With a plan you can avoid being reactionary, jumping from fire, to fire to fire and finding yourself never getting ahead.

Stephen Covey who wrote *The Seven Habits of Highly Effective People* is a great mentor on time management. One of the most critical habits that he states is, "always begin with the end in mind." If you're letting the system manage you, you're never going to be able to manage the system. What do you want this to look like? Get your time in alignment with your energy which will allow you to get the maximum return on the property. Make sure to be proactive. Plan out your month, week, and day. Say, "Okay, if I do this and this, that will move me towards my end goal?" For more information on time management and beginning with the end in mind, you can read our book, *Finding and Financing Apartment Buildings: Proven Ways to Get It Done* found at Amazon.

Hopefully you now have a much clearer understanding of how to manage apartment buildings for fun and profit. We hope that by sharing our expertise and experience you will be better prepared for what is ahead.

Have a great day!

CLOSING

We have enjoyed sharing our thoughts and experiences related to taking over and managing your apartment buildings. We hope our information will help you move toward a successful apartment investing career.

For additional information, you may want to read our other book: _Finding and Financing Apartment Buildings: Proven Ways to Get It Done_ which is available at Amazon.

www.ingramcontent.com/pod-product-compliance
Lightning Source LLC
Chambersburg PA
CBHW030654220526
45463CB00005B/1766